C   D I A

RECOR
BREAKER

Legendary Feats by Canada's Greatest Play

J. Alexander Poulton

OVER TIME BOOKS

© 2004 by Éditions de la Montagne Verte

10 9 8 7 6 5 4 3 2 1

Printed in Canada

The Publisher: OverTime Books is an imprint of Éditions de la Montagne Verte

Library and Archives Canada Cataloguing in Publication

Poulton, J. Alexander (Jay Alexander)

Canadian hockey record breakers : legendary feats by
   Canada's greatest players / J. Alexander Poulton.

Includes bibliographical references.

ISBN 0-9737681-0-X

   1. Hockey—Canada—History. 2. Hockey players—Canada.
I. Title.

GV848.5.A1P69 2005   796.962'0971   C2005-901491-1

Project Director: J. Alexander Poulton
Project Editor: Joel Semchuk

Cover Image: Wayne Gretzky. Courtesy of Getty Images. Photo by
Bruce Bennett
Title Page: Gordie Howe and Pat Quinn. Courtesy of Graphic Artists
/Hockey Hall of Fame

PC: P6

Table of Contents

Dedication

To my parents, for everything.

Acknowledgements

I owe an enormous thank you to Peter Boer; a great friend, a great writer and a fellow hockey aficionado. Many thank yous go to my publisher for giving me the chance to have my voice heard. My father, I thank for the memories of those games spent together. To my mother, brother and my entire family, thank you for the support and fun we have together. To the Garceau family, thanks simply for being there. To all my friends, thank you for your support and for listening to all the hockey stories. Thanks to Manny Almela, for sharing those war stories. And finally, my gratitude to all hockey fans, like myself, who keep the fires burning for their favourite teams while we wait for the next season to begin. Go Habs Go!!!

"Winning does solve everything."
–Joe Sakic, Colorado Avalanche.

Introduction

The legends have been made, the mythologies have grown, and new heroes continue to emerge from a country that lives, breathes and dies by the exploits of the Canadian men and women who call the hockey rink their home.

Ever since I saw my first hockey game, I have been glued to the exploits of the people who play my favourite sport. I can remember Saturday nights when my father took me to the Montréal Forum. The Atwater metro would be packed with fans streaming out onto the streets under the neon lights that outlined the escalators of the Forum that looked like two giant hockey sticks ready to take a face-off.

My dad and I would make our way through the standing room only section to our seats, ready for the Canadiens to come bursting out of the dressing room and onto the ice. It was a rite of passage for any boy growing up in Montréal to be taken to the Forum and watch the Habs play; the ice had seen so many moments that have come to define why I love the game so much.

It is because of my passion for hockey that I present you this look into some of the most legendary moments in the history of Canadian hockey. I have added my own interpretation of certain events; I felt this was a necessary step to make the mountains of statistical data a little easier on the reader.

This book is a look back to the players and moments that have defined Canadian hockey over the past 100 years, and they are the moments we all remember: Henderson scoring the winning goal of the Summit Series, Gretzky's 50 goals in 39 games, the Richard Riot of 1954. These are moments that brought people together and occasionally moments that tore them apart.

In the record books are names like "Phantom" Joe Malone who, playing for the 1920s Québec Bulldogs, scored seven goals in one game. And Maurice "Rocket" Richard, who was the first to score 50 goals in a season. Yet, these records do not even begin to illustrate the stories behind these exceptional accomplishments. The stats sheet is just one side to the history of Canadian hockey.

Ask any Montréal Canadiens fan what "Rocket" Richard means to them and they will surely have a story to tell. Ask any Edmonton Oilers fan their favourite moment and the name Wayne Gretzky will surely come to mind. These names have come to mean something greater in the world of hockey than the players' on-ice play alone. Who among us hasn't pretended to be "Rocket" Richard, Gordie Howe, or Wayne Gretzky bearing down on some poor goalie to score the Stanley Cup-winning goal, or maybe being Patrick Roy flashing the leather to snag a bullet that was destined for the top corner? We all wanted to be like those heroes of our youth, and we continue, as older children, to look on those moments for inspiration, for an escape, for the dream. Certain players have moved beyond the status of mere hockey player and have placed themselves into the history books.

Some of hockey's most legendary moments were made by players who never got the public attention of the Gretzkys or Howes of the NHL. Their careers might not stand out like others, but for one moment they held everyone's attention by scoring the winner or making the save that defined their careers as hockey players.

Say the name Paul Henderson, and any Canadian will tell you that he was the one who scored the most famous goal in hockey in the final game of the 1972 Summit Series against Russia. Few people remember that he was a solid defensive forward for the Maple Leafs who consistently delivered and always played to the best of his ability. Paul Henderson's hockey career is now defined by that one moment when he slipped the puck by Russian goalie Tretiak. That moment has come to embody Canada's national pastime and also has made a legend out of a good defensive forward.

These are the moments that all hockey players dream of. I am certain that if you were to ask Paul Henderson if he is upset that no one remembers his NHL achievements and only remembers him for his 1972 Summit Series winning goal, he would answer with a confident "No."

These legendary moments in hockey are not only restricted to the men. Canadian women's hockey has come out of the shadows and has earned the respect and financial support it lacked for so long. Dismissed at first as slow and not exciting, women's hockey has come into its own. The game is now thrilling crowds across Canada and developing its own set of players who have made significant contributions to that sport. Look no further than players like Hayley Wickenheiser. The Canadian Women's National Team has won eight World Championship titles.

To the hockey fan, these players are heroes that we grew up with, the players into which we invested our passions and hopes, yet none of these players would ever call themselves a legend. Rocket Richard, who means as much to Montréal Canadiens fans now as he did when he played, remained as humble as ever and never claimed to be anything more than a simple hockey player. He said he achieved those things not because of any special power or knowledge, but with a simple belief that if you work hard, the results will naturally come. As a boy, Gretzky practiced on his backyard rink until either cold or darkness made him go inside. He lived and breathed hockey.

This is the difference between the legends and the players. The legends are the ones who take that extra step regardless of the outcome—the thrill of victory or the agony of defeat.

Chapter One

THE FORWARDS
They Shoot, They Score

"Phantom" Joe Malone
The Natural

There were none before him to look up to, none before him to learn from, none before him to show him how to score. But despite the absence of role models, "Phantom" Joe Malone quickly became the player to whom future hockey stars would aspire to when they dreamed about playing professional hockey. He was fast on his skates, a gentleman on and off the ice when he had to be and he could lead a team to victory on his own by the sheer number of goals he could score.

For players in Malone's time, hockey was mostly a part-time job. Since a season normally lasted only about 20 games, most players had to have another income to support themselves for the remainder of the year. Hockey was seen as a second job in the beginning of the professional leagues. The players worked in factories, offices, government institutions and some were even recruited from the army. Before the National Hockey League established itself and brought in the attendance numbers needed to keep the franchises alive, players' salaries were a fraction of what the top players make in today's NHL.

In his second year with the Montréal Canadiens, like many other players Malone only played eight home games because he could not afford to lose a job he'd landed in Québec City. He knew from the dissolution of the National Hockey Association and many other local leagues that hockey wasn't yet a proven business and that he would need a second job to support his family.

"I had hooked on to a good job in Québec City which promised a secure future, something hockey in those days couldn't," said Malone as he recalled days when players' salaries peaked at the princely sum of $800 per season. "We mostly played for the love of the game," remarked Malone. "Guys would get injured, and it ended up that they couldn't work. But we kept coming back. Foolish, some might say, but we loved every second of it!"

The men who started it all played for the love of the game. After the games there were no fans waiting to get autographs, no player agents, no million-dollar salaries and definitely no unions. Players might have received a gratuity from the team's business sponsors, but earnings still remained small. Nevertheless, as the game spread to communities across Canada, organized leagues began to spring up as communities faced off against each other for hockey bragging rights. It wasn't until the formation of the National Hockey League in 1917 that some players could make a decent living from hockey.

⊷◆⊶

Born Maurice Joseph Malone in Québec City on February 28, 1890, Malone was attracted to hockey from an early age. He watched the older kids strap on their makeshift skates at the local patch of frozen water. They then cleared off a section, forming the sideboards by patting down snow until it made a nice hard surface. Since they sometimes couldn't find pucks, they would make do with any little piece of rubber, wood or whatever could be fashioned into a round projectile. There was no strategy or fancy passing. It was everybody against one player, and Malone learned quickly. The winner was basically whoever could hold onto the puck the longest. Using his natural speed, Malone often left a pack of tired kids behind him.

It was the same thing when you watched him play years later for the Canadiens. Malone guarded the puck like he had a pack of puck-hungry kids trying to take away his prize. He could skate through any roadblock and score with a precise snap of the wrists into the back of the net. His was a pure style of hockey that wasn't fancy but got the job done better than anyone else in his time.

Urged on by his father, Malone joined his first organized league at the age of 17, playing for the Québec Crescents of the Québec Amateur Athletics Association. However, it wasn't until Malone joined the Québec Bulldogs of the National Hockey Association that people began to take notice of this skater that could hit as hard as guys twice his size and still skate circles around them. At 177 cm tall and weighing 68 kilograms, Malone quickly earned the respect of other players who at first were quick to dismiss the diminutive forward. He was aptly given the nickname "Phantom" for his speed and his lethal instinct around the net. Opposing players were often left dead in their tracks as the Phantom skated directly toward them but somehow seemed to move right through them. Other players could skate as fast as Malone, but none seemed to have the ability to move with the puck like he could.

The rules of the NHA forced Malone to develop a certain style to his game. Since forward passing was not allowed, Malone's style of holding onto the puck and making his way from one end of the ice to the other was almost a necessity. The skills he had learned on the pond as a kid were coming in handy. It was a different game in Malone's time, and he was the best at it.

By the 1912–13 season Malone firmly established his place among the elite players in the small NHA league. In just 20 games, Malone scored 43 goals, and in one game on March 8, 1913, he scored nine goals during the Stanley Cup challenge series. With his prolific scoring, Malone led the way for his team to take home their first NHA championship and the highly sought-after Stanley Cup. Malone and the Bulldogs carried the energy from this Stanley Cup-winning season into the next and won another cup, with Malone scoring just 24 goals in 17 regular season games. Unfortunately, the team would never hoist the Stanley Cup over their heads again, but Malone was just getting started on his record-setting career.

In 1917, when the National Hockey League was formed, the financially strapped Québec Bulldogs could not afford to keep the franchise in the city and was forced to send its players off to the league's other teams. The Montréal Canadiens wisely signed Malone to the team, and his contributions showed immediately. With his new line mates, legends Newsy Lalonde and Didier Pitre, Malone had the best season of his career and established a goal-scoring record that wasn't broken until another Montréal Canadiens star came along 27 years later.

With World War I taking so many talented players out of hockey and owners becoming increasingly desperate to get more fans into the empty seats, a goal scorer like Malone was a welcome addition for the Canadiens. As word spread of his talents on the ice, local news headlines shouted their approval: "Malone scores 5! Canadiens win 6–4!" "Malone wins game on his own!" "The Phantom strikes again!" The seats began to fill up with curious people looking to see this newest hockey sensation. Malone and his line mates wasted no time in giving the public and the papers something to talk about.

The hockey of Malone's time was rough, fast and high scoring. It was not abnormal to have games with totals in the double digits. (The NHL record for most goals scored by a team in a single game: Montréal Canadiens versus Malone's new team, the Québec Bulldogs; the Canadiens won 16–3.) There were no zones on the ice; forward passing was not allowed; and goaltenders were not allowed to drop to their knees to make a save, making for an offensive-minded approach to the game. A minor penalty cost players three minutes, not the two minutes of today's game, allowing extra time for a power play goal. Another rule that helped the goal scorers was that goaltenders had to serve their own penalties, meaning a forward or defenceman would take over in the net until the penalty expired, allowing players like Malone to take advantage of these inexperienced net minders.

Scoring came easily for Malone that season. It was not uncommon for him to score a hat trick in one game and the next day score five points. He won games on his own, once even scoring all four goals in a win over Toronto (4–0). With Lalonde and Pitre on his side, Malone went on to finish the season with a record-setting 44 goals in 20 games, an average of 2.2 goals per game. Unfortunately, Malone's scoring prowess wasn't enough—the

Canadiens were defeated in the Stanley Cup finals by the Toronto Arenas.

Looking at the record, it seems almost impossible in the context of today's game for a player to even come close to scoring 44 goals in 20 games. Yet, Malone's record came at a time when the rules allowed for a more open game that benefited the goal scorers. This does not in any way diminish the scoring machine that Malone was; it serves to illustrate how he came to score so many goals in such a limited number of games.

Despite the different rules and different style of the game, Malone's record for the most goals in a single NHL season seemed unattainable; a record that would stand the test of time...until Maurice "Rocket" Richard came along in the 40s. Richard broke Malone's record and established a new one— 50 goals in 50 games.

After an abbreviated season in 1918–19 with the Canadiens, Malone returned to Québec City and joined his old Bulldog team that just re-entered the NHL for the 1919–20 season. The glory days of the old team were not there this time, however, and the Bulldogs ended the season with a dismal four wins and 20 losses. Although his team did not have the success it previously enjoyed when it was part of the National Hockey Association, Malone again became the stand-out player in the league, netting 39 goals in 24 games. The shining moment of that season came on January 31, 1920, when the

Bulldogs took on their rivals from Ontario, the Toronto St. Patricks.

Before a sparse crowd of only 1200 people, the animosity between the two teams began to heat up early as sticks and bodies flew all over the ice. The Bulldogs and the St. Pats fought up and down both ends of the ice, but it was Malone who got the first goal on a brilliant rush down the left wing, snapping a shot in the right-hand corner of the net. Later in the period, with his teammates crowded in front of the net, Malone let loose another shot that found the back of the net but was immediately recalled by the referee. Apparently, in the mess of arms and legs, the referee saw that the puck was kicked in. Malone knew he'd scored. Furious over the disallowed goal, Malone doubled his efforts for the second and third periods.

The Bulldogs pulled away in the second period, moving up on the Toronto team 6–4 with Malone scoring two more goals. It wasn't until late in the third period with the Bulldogs leading by one goal that Malone scored three unanswered goals. He ended the game with a total of seven goals, and the Bulldogs won the game 10–6. The win wasn't important to the team; the Bulldogs were clearly not going to make the playoffs. Although that season was a disaster, Malone established a record that has yet to be broken. A few have come close to beating it, but Malone still stubbornly holds a record that at the time meant little to him. He had already scored nine goals in an NHA playoff game in 1913, so scoring seven didn't seem like much to him. But, it is the record that still stands today as a mark to beat.

"I was just playing a game that I loved. The stats never mattered to me that much," Malone recalled.

After two seasons in Québec and Hamilton, Malone was dealt back to the Montréal Canadiens. Whether the game changed or Malone lost his touch as a goal scorer, he scored only one goal in his last two seasons with the Canadiens before he finally retired in 1924. He finished his career with a total of 146 goals in 124 games, scoring five or more goals in a single game 10 times. Although he didn't end on his highest note, Joe Malone had an extraordinary career that established him as one of the legends of the game who laid foundations for future stars. His accomplishments were forever solidified in the annals of hockey history when "Phantom" Joe Malone was inducted into the Hockey Hall of Fame in 1950.

Maurice "Rocket" Richard
The People's Hockey Player

He knew it wouldn't be easy. After breaking his ankle and his hand in the Québec Senior Hockey League, would the team he dreamed about playing for, the team of his heroes Aurele Joliat, Howie Morenz and Georges Vezina, take a chance on a brittle kid from Montréal?

With World War II in full swing and many of the NHL players off in Europe battling Germans, young Maurice Richard knew his chance had come to show the coach what he could do and earn his spot playing for the famous "bleu, blanc, rouge."

"I'm lucky. A lot of the men have gone to war. There aren't many players left. That's why they are letting me have my turn," Maurice said to himself as he prepared to show the coaches what he could bring to the team.

The scouting reports all said the same thing: young Maurice has the talent, the speed, and most of all, the determination to play the game on a professional level. But the one thing that's holding him back is his small frame, which tended to break when taken to the boards. General Manager Tommy Gorman and Coach Dick Irvin knew that despite his fragile frame, the kid had fire in his eyes and a determination to win that could one day make him a leader on the team.

Still unsure whether Richard would hold up against the much bigger players, Coach Irvin decided during training camp to test the young forward's resolve. He assigned the task to Murph Chamberlain, a Montréal forward with a knack for hitting, to see if Richard had what it took to stand up to a little punishment. Chamberlain proceeded to run the rookie hard into the boards. Right after Maurice got up from the ice, he went straight for Chamberlain ready to solve their differences with his fists clenched tightly. It took three teammates to remove Maurice from his large inquisitor. Right then, Irvin knew he had something to work with, and he signed Richard to a two-year contract.

Walking into the great Forum for the first time as a Montréal Canadien and looking at the pictures of his boyhood heroes, Maurice arrived where he had long dreamed of when he was a young boy playing hockey in the streets of his Montréal neighbourhood. As he laced up his skates for his first game against the Boston Bruins, Richard sat beside legends Elmer Lach and Toe Blake. Richard strained to understand the coach's English as the man laid out his game plan against the hard-hitting Bruins. Maurice knew his first game would not be easy, but he welcomed the challenge and the chance to show all the doubters what he could do. For the game, he was teamed up with centre Elmer Lach and right-winger Tony Demers on the second line.

Also starting that night in a Canadiens uniform were veterans Gord Drillion and Dutch Hiller, who had been added to the team to shore up an offence that hadn't been putting up the numbers during the regular season. The Bruins were fully aware of all the new additions to the Canadiens line-up and focused their game strategy on containing the new players. The Bruins' attack was relentless, and they held the top line scoreless for the first period. However, it turned out that the Bruins chose the wrong line to shadow, allowing Richard, Demers and Lach more opportunities to manoeuvre. Maurice loved to play this type of game because it allowed the speedy forward to gain momentum through the neutral zone and carry his line mates over the blue as they made their way hard to the net. It was just a matter of time before Richard's line put a point on the scoreboard.

In his first game against the Boston Bruins on October 31, 1942, Richard got his first point when he and line mate Elmer Lach set up Tony Demers for a goal on their way to a 3–2 victory. It was only an assist, but it drove Richard to want to score that first goal even more. After the game, as the team packed up and his teammates congratulated him on his first NHL game, Richard thought that he had done well but would only be satisfied when he put a puck in the back of the net himself. But he would have to wait for his first goal. A customs agent denied Richard entry into the United States for the next game in New York because of a visa problem. Frustrated, Maurice saved his energy for the next game. His first goal of many came a few days later on November 8, 1942, when the Rangers visited the Montréal Forum.

Maurice knew the pressure was on him to show the Montréal crowd what he could do. Montréal had not seen the Stanley Cup since 1931, and the sparse crowd at the Rangers game told Maurice that he would have to work hard to win over the notorious Montréal fans. It would be a tough sell, since the last player to hold the attention of the Montréal fans was the great Howie Morenz. A fan favourite, Morenz was able to captivate the crowd with one move of his stick. Maurice was well aware of the glorious past that had skated before him, but he knew that this was his time to come out of the shadows and show the crowd that he could bring back those days when the Forum erupted at the exploits of its favourite players.

The fans knew that they had something after Richard's first goal of his National Hockey League career. It came early in the second period when Maurice, playing left wing, picked up the puck behind Canadiens goalie Paul Bibeault's net. Wearing the number 15 at the time, Richard gazed at the other end of the ice and saw his path through to the goalie. With a skating stride that eventually earned him the nickname "Rocket," Maurice flew past the unprepared Rangers, bouncing off anyone who tried to get in his way. Nothing could stop him as he put his head down, his trademark coal-black eyes staring directly at the last man between him and his first NHL goal. Before the Rangers defence had time to react, Maurice was in front of Rangers goaltender Steve Buzinski and put a backhand in the top corner. The crowd was on its feet, cheering for the player they had longed hoped would take the Canadiens to new heights. Maurice wasted no time gaining more fans. On November 22, 1942, he scored his first hat trick.

It wasn't until the 1943–44 season that Maurice Richard became a household name across Québec. By the beginning of the 1944–45 season, the whole hockey world began to take notice of the kid with the jet black hair and fire in the eyes who projected a determination from which a legend was born.

One day during practice, Maurice and his line mates were shooting a barrage of pucks at the net. When it came time for Maurice to let loose his trademark shot, a player screamed from the bench, "Watch out, here comes the Rocket!" A reporter at the practice overheard the nickname and published it the next day. From that moment on Richard became known as Maurice "Rocket" Richard. All that remained was for the Rocket to assure his place in the record books.

Maurice Richard was not the type of man who was content with scoring a few goals and making a simple defensive contribution to his team. When Coach Dick Irvin signed Richard, he knew he was getting a player that would be a force on the ice and could chase the records. The Rocket wasted no time chasing the records that at one time seemed impossible to break.

By the time the 1944–45 season came around, coaches across the NHL were well aware of the talents of the 23-year-old Rocket Richard. They began working on systems, theories and just about any way possible to stop the scoring threat posed by Richard. They came to the conclusion that the most effective way to stop him was to simply get him off the ice for two minutes or more by goading him into the penalty box. These tactics often worked, but they did not stop Richard from his scoring exploits, and in fact fuelled the determination that led him to break one of the most sought-after records in NHL history.

"I wanted somebody on the other team to make me work harder. When somebody was checking me closely I wanted to get away from him, and I tried all the more to get my goals. If I didn't have anyone on my back or anybody to check me, I don't think I would have accomplished all that I did," remarked Richard years later, looking back on his career.

The 1944–45 season proved to be a turning point for Richard. Twenty-seven years earlier another Montréal Canadiens forward, "Phantom" Joe Malone, scored 44 goals in 20 games (during the 1917–18 season). This record seemed unattainable, yet halfway through the 1944–45 season Richard scored 29 goals in 27 games, and people began to believe he could beat Malone's record. And so did Maurice. Now teamed with Toe Blake and Elmer Lach, aptly named the "Punch Line," they became the most effective scoring line in the NHL.

Their style of play was appropriately branded "firewagon hockey" because of their speed and ability to put the puck in the back of the net when it counted the most.

That year, Rocket Richard knew it was up to him to make good on the reputation he was building as a goal-scoring forward who would not be pushed around. The goal that made Richard stand out as one of the most amazing players in the NHL was an unforgettable point he scored against the Detroit Red Wings.

"Over the years, people have asked me whether it was true that I actually scored a goal while carrying an opponent on my back, and the answer is 'yes,'" remarked Richard.

The player in question was Detroit Red Wings defenceman Earl Siebert. The game was its usual physical game between the two teams, with the Canadiens setting the pace and Richard leading the way. Richard took up the puck in his own zone and made it through the neutral zone unhindered by the hands and sticks trying to slow his charge to the net. The last man standing in his way was defenceman Earl Siebert. As Siebert cut across the ice, he realized he couldn't get in front of Richard to stop him so he did the next best thing, which was to wrap his arms around the Rocket's shoulders in an attempt to slow Maurice down. It wasn't working; Richard simply dug his skates deeper into the ice and made his way toward the net. The crowd stared in awe as Siebert, desperate to stop

Richard, jumped on his back and tried by any means necessary to stop Richard from scoring. The sound of Richard's skates digging grooves into the ice could be heard over the hum of the awestruck Forum crowd as he bore the extra burden on his back. Richard never gave up, and the crowd loved him for it. Nothing was going to stop him from scoring.

"I felt his skates lifting off the ice and flying up in the air. I think he weighed about [95 kilograms]. I felt as if I might cave in. The goaltender moved straight out for me, and somehow I managed to jab the puck between his legs while Siebert kept riding my back!" exclaimed Richard after the game.

After the game, in the Detroit dressing room, Coach Jack Adams laid into his defenceman: "You dumb Dutchman! You go and let that Richard go…!" he screamed at Siebert.

"Listen, Mr. Adams," Siebert responded in a matter-of-fact tone, "any guy who can carry me [18.29 metres] and then out the puck into the net…well, more power to him!"

Richard's reputation was set. The goals kept coming that season; he had an outstanding performance against the Detroit Red Wings, scoring five goals, then he had three games with three goals and six games with two goals.

For his record-breaking 45th goal Richard was to meet the Toronto Maple Leafs at the Montréal Forum on February 25, 1945. A game against

Toronto for the fans and for Maurice was always a charged affair. The two cities had long been rivals because one was French and one English; they were rivals in culture, rivals in development and forever rivals in hockey.

The crowd at the Forum placed all their hopes on beating Toronto, and Maurice felt the pressure. The Leafs had to keep Richard in check because they did not want to be remembered as the team that let him break the 27-year-old record. Throughout the game, Maurice was shadowed relentlessly. Despite the extra attention, Richard managed to cut loose from the defence for a breakaway. As he raced down the right side, he cut across the middle and let loose a shot, but Leafs goalie Frank McCool grabbed the puck out of the air and dashed the hopes of the crowd that was now on its feet. The fans got what they wanted— typical Rocket flair for the dramatic with three minutes remaining in the third period.

Trailing his teammate Toe Blake on a rush into the Leafs zone, Richard remained as focused as if the score was in overtime of a game seven Stanley Cup final. Blake passed the puck to Richard who found himself in front of the net. Leafs goalie Frank McCool tried to follow the coming shot, but the Rocket caught him guessing, and with a precise snap of the wrists, shot the puck into the bottom corner of the net. Maurice "Rocket" Richard scored his 45th goal. The crowd went wild while McCool hung his head and scooped the puck off the ice.

When the game ended and the crowd calmed, Montréal Canadiens legend "Phantom" Joe Malone walked slowly out onto the ice in a show of class to the new goal-scoring tour de force. He came to congratulate Maurice on beating his record. The man that once skated up and down the same rink with a speed and accuracy that earned him the nickname "Phantom" did not look the same, but the crowd still cheered him as if he still played for their beloved team.

Malone walked over to Richard and handed him the puck that broke his record. The crowd cheered as the old hero passed the torch to the new. After the game, quote-hungry reporters surrounded Richard. In true Richard form, he was always aware that the crowds at the Forum were the true inspiration for what he did on the ice. As reporters crowded around him, Richard paused when asked if he wanted to dedicate his achievement to anyone. The Rocket thought about it and then answered, "This record honours all French-Canadians." He'd set his sights on establishing his own legend.

By March 18, 1945, during the final game of the season, the Rocket scored 49 goals. The Canadiens were taking on the Bruins that night in Boston, and Richard never admitted it but he knew that he had to score a goal that night, or it would remain a statistic that would haunt him for the rest of his career. He'd already surpassed Joe Malone's goal-scoring record, and the only remaining doubt was whether or not he could get the milestone 50th goal.

By the end of the second period, Richard had not put any numbers up on the board, and the fans in the Boston arena sensed that he would not be able to score his 50th goal. But Maurice flourished under pressure. He'd responded before when his team needed him the most and delivered the game-winning goal, such as the time he scored all five goals against the Toronto Maple Leafs in the 1944 Stanley Cup semi-finals, winning the game 5–1. But this time was different; he was doing it for the team and a little for himself.

The team knew that this was Richard's last chance, and they were going to do everything to help him reach his 50th. Rushing the Boston net for one last run, Lach and Richard burst down the right wing. Lach cut across in front of the net, trying to get Richard the puck but instead running into a Bruins defenceman. The puck disappeared from sight under the sprawled-out players. Somehow in the mad scramble of arms, legs and sticks, Richard managed to come up with the puck and he shovelled it into the back of the net for his 50th goal. Bruins goaltender Harvey Bennett immediately skated towards the referee to protest that the goal was kicked in and that there was also interference on the play when Lach crashed into the net. The referee, however, did not see the infraction, and the goal stood. The Canadiens rushed the ice and crowded around their star player. In Montréal, at the Windsor train station, fans waited for their native son to return from Boston and gave him a hero's welcome that surprised the shy, quiet Richard.

Those who had previously criticized Richard as a product of a depleted wartime hockey league now reconsidered his place in the NHL. He had just broken a record that was set by the first superstar of hockey and was well on his way to breaking more. He never did duplicate his 50-goal season, but his scoring prowess never waned. He was one of the most feared players in the NHL and the bane of goalies across the league.

Johnny Bower of the Toronto Maple Leafs said of Richard's scoring ability: "I tried to size him up, but I couldn't. He'd score on me through my legs, then another along the ice, then on one side and then on the other side. He had me going crazy. The biggest thrill of my life was when he retired."

"From the blue line in, I never saw a player as exciting as Richard," said goalie Emile Francis, who had several run-ins with the Rocket. "When he had the goalie beat, he finished it off and you had no chance to recover."

The Rocket went on to terrorize more goaltenders as he pursued his next record.

Nels Stewart, who played for the Montréal Maroons, Boston Bruins and the New York Americans, held the record for the most career goals— 324 in 15 seasons of play. However, in just his 10th season in the National Hockey League, Richard reached Stewart's record. The season began with the appropriate local media storm around the demure Montréal forward; the reporters eagerly anticipated the record-breaking moment. But as the press waited vigilantly at their typewriters hoping that the Rocket would score his 324th goal, Richard went the first six games of the new season without scoring once.

On November 8, 1946, the Canadiens took on the Chicago Blackhawks at the Montréal Forum. The local press was practicing its clichés for how to write up the record-breaker in the morning paper. Another added source of news writing fodder handed to the writers like a gift was that it was the 10th anniversary of Maurice Richard's first goal with the Canadiens. The local press revelled in the moment. The headlines would read: "The Rocket blasts past Stewart," "Rocket Power Does it Again!" The crowd hustled into the Forum, ready for their hero to break another record. As the Blackhawks took to the ice, the fans greeted them with a chorus of boos. The fans were not going to make it easy for the team that would try and deny their hero from breaking the record that he deserved.

The game started out brutally, with the players feeding off the energy of the crowd. The Blackhawks relentlessly shadowed the Rocket, hoping that they wouldn't become another statistic in Richard's history. They boxed him in and assigned two players to shadow his every move. They hooked, grabbed, slashed and used everything they could throw at him to stop him from getting that point. The Montréal faithful knew that this strategy could not beat the Rocket; they'd seen it countless times before. A team would pester him all game, but the Rocket always came through on top. It was no different for the Blackhawks this time. As the fans continuously chanted "Rocket! Rocket!" he knew he couldn't fail.

Richard had a few chances to score early on in the match but to no avail as goaltender Al Rollins' determination was stronger than Richard's first five shots. With Chicago up 1–0, the Canadiens forwards began to press hard on the Blackhawks defence. Lach, Olmstead and Richard swooped in on their opponents. Rocket finally got a pass at the top of the circle and let loose a powerful shot that headed straight for the bottom corner of the net. Rollins threw out his leg and stopped the puck, but he left a big, juicy rebound for Lach to score his 200th career goal. The Forum fans gave Lach a respectful round of applause, but they were there to see their Rocket score his record-breaking goal. So, they quickly returned to their seats and waited for the moment to come.

After a quick line change, the Richard line was back on the ice. The puck dropped, and it fell back to Canadiens defenceman Butch Bouchard. He looked up the ice and found the Rocket open for a pass. Richard dug his skates in, glared forward, made his way around the Blackhawks' line and headed for the net. But the Rocket could not get by one defenceman who checked him hard into the boards. Before he fell to the ice, Richard managed to get off a weak backhand that slowly made its way toward the net. Seeing the puck's trajectory, Olmstead rushed it in an attempt to slide it past the sprawling Blackhawks goaltender. As he was about to touch the puck, a Blackhawks defenceman dragged Olmstead to the ice, and they went crashing into the net. Somehow, the puck managed to find its way past the goalie and crossed the red line. Goal! But was it Richard's goal or had Olmstead touched the puck last? The crowd collectively held its breath, waiting for the referee to point to the last person to touch the puck. Referee Red Storey immediately pointed to the Rocket. The crowd went wild; their hero had done it again. As Richard got up off the ice, he looked in the net and realized that he just broke Nels Stewart's career goals record. It hadn't been the kind of goal that he hoped to break the record with, but it got the job done. Richard bowed to the crowd, and they cheered for their local hero. The Canadiens went on to win the game 2–1.

As the team headed back to the dressing room to celebrate their victory and their star forward's record, they noticed that someone had taken their frustrations out on the room. Olmstead was the first in the room, and had vented his anger on the bags and wastebaskets for not having been awarded a goal that he knew was his.

Earlier, after the Richard goal, when Olmstead lined up for the final face-off, a Chicago player asked him, "Why didn't you tell them it was your goal? We all saw from the bench that you had touched it last." To which Olmstead replied, "I'd get shot if I did!"

What was left for the Rocket now that he had broken Joe Malone's single season goal record and Nels Stewart's most career goals record? Maurice Richard would continue to astound hockey fans around the league, and especially in Montréal, with his dynamic play. He became a hero to a new generation of hockey fans, all of whom grew up wearing their number nine jerseys, dreaming about playing in the NHL and scoring a goal like Maurice Richard for the Montréal Canadiens. He was able like no other player to score a goal when the team needed it, and in the most dramatic fashion possible. He moved the fans of Montréal not just as a player but also as a man who always gave respect to the people who supported him and who always remembered where he came from. He appreciated every bit of support he got but never did get used to the attention that seemed to follow him everywhere.

"He could rile up the Montréal fans in a hurry," recalled Gordie Howe. "God, sometimes I felt sorry for the man. He must have got a standing ovation when he went shopping."

The applause never ceased, and for the rest of his career, Richard would be the one setting records that future hockey stars would seek to break.

Gordie Howe
Mr. Hockey

Would he ever play the game again?

With a top line of Gordie Howe, Ted Lindsay and Sid Abel, the Red Wings finally looked like they had a chance to win the 1950 Stanley Cup (in the 1949–50 season) after several years at the bottom of the league. These players gave the Wings an offensive threat that they needed in order to secure a chance at the Stanley Cup. Gordie Howe finished the year with 35 goals and 33 assists, putting him third on the scoring list right behind fellow line mates Lindsay and Abel. The line was ready to take on the Toronto Maple Leafs in the first round of the playoffs when disaster struck.

The Toronto Maple Leafs had a lot on the line. They were the defending Stanley Cup Champions, and they could not lose in the first round to the younger, upstart Red Wings squad whom they had beaten in the playoffs for the past two years. The Leafs came out hitting hard and aggressively fore-checked the puck carrier. The Maple Leafs' game strategy was to hold the line of Howe, Lindsay and Abel to a minimum of points, shadowing their every move. Toronto Captain Ted Kennedy was given the difficult task of shadowing the speedy Howe.

The Red Wings could not be contained by the Maple Leafs defence. Time and again Howe and his line mates kept breaking into the Maple Leafs' zone, getting their chances at goaltender Turk Broda. Feeling the pressure of the Red Wings offence, the Maple Leafs tried to tighten up their defence. The Leafs were having trouble all game just getting the puck out of their zone due to aggressive Red Wings fore-checking. Seeing an opportunity to break the Red Wings' hold on the game, Leafs Captain Kennedy took control of the puck and led the way out into open ice. Howe sped toward Kennedy, who was coming up along the boards, in an attempt to cut him off. Seeing the speeding Howe coming for him, Kennedy put on the brakes to avoid a certain hard check. Missing the check, Howe was sent barrelling headfirst into the boards at full speed. He hit the boards with a devastating thud that was heard throughout the arena. Everyone knew that he was not going to come out of a play like that unscathed. Players quickly gathered around as the trainers attempted to awaken the unconscious and bleeding Red Wings forward. Fearing the worst, Howe was stabilized and carried off the ice on a stretcher directly to emergency surgery.

At the hospital, doctors realized that Gordie had suffered severe head trauma so they performed a 90-minute operation to relieve pressure that was building on his brain. His injuries were diagnosed as a concussion, a fractured nose, fractured cheekbone and cut eye. The operation saved his life but ended his playoff hopes.

"He is lucky to be alive," said Dr. Tomsu, the neurosurgeon who operated on Howe, at a press conference after the surgery. "There was severe haemorrhaging and a pocket of fluid that had collected on the brain called a subdural hygroma that provided some anxious moments. But now he is out of danger."

Despite Howe's absence, the Red Wings managed to defeat the Toronto Maple Leafs and go on to win the Stanley Cup. Howe eventually recovered from his injuries and made a triumphant return to the Red Wings' line-up the next season, going on to win the overall scoring title.

The comparisons have been made countless times throughout Howe's career. When he first broke into the league in 1946, he was compared to Maurice Richard. Even after retiring from the game, the comparisons didn't stop. Ever since Wayne Gretzky broke into the NHL, the comparisons between him and Howe have continued. Who was the better player? Who has the better play-making ability? Who deserves all the praise?

Pushing all comparisons aside for the moment, Gordie Howe has a style and talent all his own. The measure of a quality hockey player is that he can put up consistent numbers year after year, and Howe did that throughout his 26 seasons of hockey, earning him the nickname "Mr. Hockey."

He won the scoring title four years in a row, the Art Ross Trophy as the league's top scorer six times and the Hart Trophy as the league's most valuable player six times. He was named to the All-Star team a record 21 times and broke all the league's top scoring records (that is, until Gretzky appeared on the scene). Howe's 49 goals in the 1952–53 season came at a time when the league was known for its overly tight defensive style. Even at the age of 41, which is considered old by hockey standards, Howe continued to produce and scored 44 goals and 59 assists, breaking the 100-point mark for the first time in his career.

The first NHL record Howe set out to break was the difficult career goal total set by Maurice Richard (at 544). Even though it took Howe 154 extra games to beat Richard's record, Howe continued to score goals at a consistent pace. Gordie ended up setting the bar at 801 goals when he scored his final goal as a member of the Hartford Whalers in 1980 at the amazing age of 51. As the goal totals went up over Howe's career, he reached several astonishing plateaus.

Known as much for his skating as for his scoring ability, Howe was also not one to shy away from any challenge and could deliver a bone-crushing check as good as the toughest guys in the league. Several times Howe was known to quickly dispose of some challenger who was ignorant as to his skills in the not-so-subtle aspect of the game when the gloves fall to the ice.

However, all those body checks began to wear on Howe, who collected some 300 stitches, damaged knees, an assortment of broken bones, a dislocated shoulder and the near-death experience in the

1950 playoffs. When the 1971 season ended, Gordie Howe announced his retirement from the NHL because of the limitations that his injuries put on his game. The normal Hall of Fame inductee waiting time was waved, and Howe became a member in 1972.

Mr. Hockey could not stay away from the game he loved for long, and at the age of 45 Howe joined the World Hockey Association. He quickly regained his amazing form and scored 100 points in the 1973–74 season. After six seasons in the WHA, Howe returned to the ranks of the National Hockey League and played a full 80-game season with the Hartford Whalers. He contributed a respectable 15 goals and 21 assists at the age of 51 before retiring again in 1980. He played regular professional hockey over an amazing five decades...six including a 40-second shift with the Detroit Vipers of the International Hockey League at the age of 69. Gordie Howe truly lived up to the name "Mr. Hockey."

As for all the comparisons...,the numbers provide an answer as to who has the most points. But on looking beyond the numbers, Gordie Howe was considered the best hockey player of his time. He was a consistent player who could score goals at one end of the ice and then rush back to defend his territory. You simply could not have an NHL career total of 801 goals and 1049 assists in 1760 games and not be considered one of the greatest players to ever lace up a pair of skates.

Darryl Sittler
The Year of His Life

During his first two years with the Toronto Maple Leafs, Darryl Sittler did not get the début he wanted, scoring only 25 goals. But in the 1973–74 season, Sittler turned things around and became one of the top players in the NHL at the time.

A few years later (in 1976) Sittler had his best year in the NHL. The first highlight for the Maple Leafs forward came on February 7, 1976, when the Toronto Maple Leafs took on the Boston Bruins. No special attention was brought to the game; it was just a regular season match-up between two teams who were fighting for a favourable position in the coming playoffs. Boston had the upper hand on the Leafs that season, but this game would prove to be different.

From the moment the puck was dropped it was clear that the Leafs had the game under control. Boston could not get a play started, and the Leafs pounded the Bruins' net with shot after shot. Sittler really led the game, scoring six goals and assisting four: a record that has survived even the Gretzky and Lemieux years.

Recalling the game, Sittler said: "As much as the fans fault Reece for what happened, it was simply a night where every shot and pass I made seemed to pay off in a goal. I hit the corners a couple of times, banking shots in off the post. The kid was screened on a couple of goals and had no chance.

He didn't really flub one goal. On the 10th point I banked a shot in from behind the net off Brad Park's leg."

The Leafs handed the Boston Bruins one of their most embarrassing losses of the season and also shattered the confidence of Boston rookie goal-tender Dave Reece, who was unfortunately dubbed "In-the-wrong-place-at-the-wrong-time-Reece."

In the playoffs that year, Sittler played another game that went down in the record books. In the first round of the playoffs the Leafs were taking on the tough Philadelphia Flyers and the excellent goaltending of Bernie Parent. The hard checking of the Flyers and the solid goaltending of Parent did not stop Sittler from having another memo-rable game. He scored five goals to tie an NHL record. Unfortunately, the Leafs would not make it any further in the playoffs, but Sittler's banner year was far from over.

He later secured his place in the history books during the first Canada Cup, when Team Canada found itself in overtime against Czechoslovakia. After a back and forth game, the two teams could not break the 4–4 tie, making overtime necessary to decide who won the first-ever Canada Cup. With national pride on the line, Canada battled to get the puck past the Czechoslovakian net minder but could not break the deadlock until the 11th minute of the first overtime period. Sittler proved to be the hero again when he picked up the puck at centre ice and streaked down on the left side. The Montréal Forum crowd could sense something coming as Sittler broke through the defence, and with a slight deke, put the puck past the outstretched Czechoslovakian goalie for the winning goal.

Although Sittler would never win a Stanley Cup, he continued to lead the Leafs to several successful seasons. They came close in the 1978 playoffs, only to be eliminated in the semi-finals. After 16 seasons in the NHL Sittler finished his career with 1121 total points and was inducted into the Hockey Hall of Fame in 1989.

Wayne Gretzky
The Greatest One

The −20°C wind whipped across the backyard, blowing snow into large drifts on the ice. Every half hour he got out his dad's shovel to clear the snow from the ice so that he could continue to practice the game he loved.

"Walter, do you think it's okay if Wayne stays out there all day? You know, he might catch cold," Phyllis said in a motherly tone, looking out the kitchen window at her son shooting pucks into the empty net.

"He's fine out there," replied Walter. "He plays his first game in a couple of weeks, and besides, he won't come in. I already asked him."

From an early age, the Gretzky family knew that young Wayne had a special talent when it came to hockey. He put on his first pair of skates at the age of two and quickly learned the subtleties of the game on the backyard rink (dubbed Wally Coliseum) that his father built for him in his Brantford, Ontario suburban home.

In Wayne Gretzky's first year playing organized hockey he only managed to score one goal. But his coach found the young player after the game and uttered a few words that seem rather amusing in retrospect: "You'll score a lot more than this, but here's the first one."

Before entering into his teens, young Wayne Gretzky was already breaking records and gaining the attention of the hockey world around him. In just one season, Wayne scored an amazing 378 goals in just 82 games. At only 132 cm, Wayne could never play the physical game that many other, larger kids were being taught to play by their coaches. Fortunately, Wayne looked at hockey in a different way. Walter always taught him that the player who could see several moves ahead of the opponent always had the advantage even if he was much smaller. Gretzky practiced drill after drill on his backyard rink, skating, shooting and visualizing how the game was played, trying to perfect his strategy. Sometimes his father braved the cold weather to practice with his son, teaching him the few things he knew about the game.

"People say you can't teach visualization," said Walter Gretzky in Peter Gzowski's book *The Game of Our Lives*. "I'm not so sure. I used to get them out on the ice and I'd shoot the puck down the boards toward a corner and I'd say 'Chase that.' Well, they'd all go right into the end after it. Then I'd say, 'Wait, watch me.' I'd shoot it in again, and let it roll around the net. Instead of following it around the boards I'd cut across to where it was rolling. 'There,' I'd say. 'You've got to know where it's going to go.'"

All the practice seemed to pay off; the young phenomenon continued to amass points and break every record previously set. Soon the media got wind of the exploits of a skinny kid in small-town Ontario that could score goals and make a play like the great Gordie Howe. Soon small-town arenas began to fill up with curious onlookers hoping to catch a glimpse of the young star's talents. Being in the spotlight was not something Gretzky was used to. During one exhibition game where a large crowd gathered to see him, the 10-year-old went through the motions and did not put any effort into his game. Wayne was about to learn another lesson from his father that stayed with him for the rest of his life.

"My father said, 'I don't ever want to see you do that again. All these people came to see you play. You have to be at your top level every night, whether it's an exhibition game or game seven!'" said Gretzky, looking back at that defining moment in his life. "That always stuck with me. I knew then that I was on display."

Throughout all the years, Wayne Gretzky has rarely disappointed both on and off the ice. From the backyard rink to the National Hockey League, Wayne used those lessons to become one of the greatest all-round players and one of the most prolific record breakers in National Hockey League history.

Like all stars, Gretzky collected his fair share of criticism entering into the NHL. A lot of good things were being written about him as well, but it was the few voices of discontent that ate away at the thin-skinned Gretzky. He was too small, too frail; he won't be able to score against a professional team…and so on. They all echoed the same thing, and Gretzky quickly silenced the critics in his first year with the new Edmonton Oilers. He scored 51 goals and 86 assists for a total of 137 points, and he was just getting started. Sure, he wasn't big enough, strong enough, or even fast enough to do what he wanted to do. Gretzky's talent was to put his opponents' focus entirely on him, which made the rest of the team a bigger threat. For other superstars, the challenge for the team was to get the puck to the Richards and Howes of the league because they were the ones who could carry the puck and put it into the net using their individual skills. The league quickly learned what made Gretzky such a threat but it could do little to stop him and his teammates from changing the way the game was played.

Gretzky did it time and time again. After creating a momentary distraction he passed the puck off to another player and then he'd sneak into the zone unnoticed to set up behind the net. That area colourfully came to be known as his office, where size and strength didn't matter. Behind the net with his eyes uncharacteristically pointed down, Gretzky distinguished his teammates by the colour of their hockey pants so he wouldn't have to look up and take his eyes off the puck. This made it harder for the other team to figure out where he would pass the puck next, establishing an offensive aspect to the game that allowed more goals and a more exciting game for fans to watch. The National Hockey League hadn't seen this type of open hockey since the days of Maurice Richard and Gordie Howe in the 40s and early 50s.

Gretzky's 61 (held or shared) National Hockey League scoring records and the sheer enormity of the numbers made him the most dominant player in all North American team sports. The first and most significant of the records Gretzky broke was in his second season with the Oilers. He was quickly approaching Phil Esposito's single season record for total points well before the end of the 1980–81 season.

After his first stellar season, the criticisms that initially hung over Wayne Gretzky's head began to fade as he kicked off his second season with the Edmonton Oilers. The skinny kid from Brantford was proving himself to be a proficient scorer and a natural leader on a team made up of several young prospects. That season, Gretzky played several three goal-games, one with four and one game against the St. Louis Blues where he scored five goals and two assists. Game by game, he proved his critics wrong. By the end of the season, Gretzky scored 55 goals and 109 assists for a total of 164 points. In just his second season with the Edmonton Oilers Gretzky broke Bobby Orr's record of 102 assists in a season (set in 1970–71), and he broke Phil Esposito's record of 152 points in a single season (also in 1970–71). Soon after the end of the season, Gretzky's star began to rise, and it only became bigger as he moved into the next big season of his hockey career.

During the 1981–82 hockey season, Gretzkymania exploded across the hockey world and beyond. Just before his 21st birthday in January, Gretzky scored 50 goals in just 39 games, which was 11 fewer games than the 50 goals in 50 games record that is shared by Maurice Richard and Mike Bossy, and he did it in the most exciting fashion possible. Ever since the Rocket set the mark in 1945, 50 goals in 50 games remained one of hockey's most mythical barriers. Averaging one goal per game was hard enough; Gretzky simply destroyed that mark.

On December 30, 1981, the Edmonton Oilers met the Philadelphia Flyers for a regular season game that nobody expected would be a history-making event. The media certainly was not expecting anything to come out of the game, since Gretzky was still five goals away from breaking the 50 in 50 record and was unlikely to get there until the New Year.

Philly was a team that the Oilers loved to play. The American team threw all kinds of hits, body checks, clutches and grabs but nothing worked on the speedy Oilers team. The Flyers played a bruising style of hockey that earned them the nickname "The Broad Street Bullies," and they had little chance against the emerging dominance of the Oilers' scoring machine. With a few minutes remaining in the third period, both the crowd and Gretzky knew he had a chance at beating the Richard-Bossy record. Gretzky scored four goals on Philly goaltender Pete Peeters and the net was empty as Philadelphia pulled their goalie in a last-ditch effort to tie the game and send it into over-time. As time ticked away, tension in the arena began to build, and Gretzky stepped out onto the ice hoping to get hold of the puck. With a minute remaining, the puck finally found its way onto his stick. As he skated down the ice, the crowd was cheering for him as loud as they could, which was an accomplishment in and of itself since the Oilers were playing in Philly that night. As Gretzky pulled his stick back and released the puck toward the empty net, the crowd began cheering for him even before the puck hit the back of the net. After the game, the media swarmed around an over-whelmed Gretzky and shot question after question at the young star.

"Gretzky! Wayne! What does it feel like to break such a coveted record?" barked one reporter.

"Now that you have 50 goals in 39 games, do you think you'll break Esposito's 76 regular season goals? You seem to be on pace to do so," asked one sportswriter hoping for a headline.

Through it all, Gretzky tried to downplay the moment. "To hit 76, I'd have to get 26 goals in 40 games," he said. "Never mind what's happened up 'til now; that's a lot of goals. I still have a long way to go, and I will not make any predictions. Now, if you guys will excuse me I have to call my dad."

Despite what he told reporters Gretzky had much more to give that season, and by the end, he'd set a few more records. He ended up finishing the season with a record 92 goals, 120 assists and 212 points; the first player ever to break the 200-point mark.

Looking back on the records, Gretzky pondered which future stars might equal or break some records.

"Ninety-two goals can fall," he said with a bemused smile on his face. "If a guy stays healthy and he's on the right team, he could break that one. Fifty in 39 games will be a tough one to beat since a guy would have to score an average of more than a goal a game."

After the record-setting 1981–82 season, Gretzky knew that he was the centre of attention in the hockey world. That year his team set an NHL record—the team to score the most goals at 424. Also, several Oilers topped the scoring list with Messier potting 50 goals, Kurri scoring 32 and Glen Anderson with a point total of 105. They all deserve attention for a team that was changing the face of hockey, but it was number 99 that the fans and media wanted. The image of Gretzky began to define hockey in the 80s—number 99, with his sweater tucked in on one side, gliding down through centre ice. He would veer off to the wing, still holding the puck and waiting for what seemed like an eternity for the play to catch up. As he glanced over the ice, his mind worked through the game. Would he pass or shoot? He could easily put the puck directly on a teammate's stick or find a small enough opening for the puck to squeeze by the goalie. With his natural talent and a great team to back him up, milestones just kept coming for the Great One.

After winning four Stanley Cups with the Edmonton Oilers, Gretzky established himself as the city's favourite adopted son. The fans knew that they had the privilege of watching one of the best players in NHL history play for their team, and he led the Oilers to four Stanley Cups. As summer was coming to a close and Edmonton fans looked forward to another year of hockey and maybe another Stanley Cup led by their captain, a darkness began to form over the city. On August 8, 1988, a press conference was called at Molson House.

As a nervous and teary-eyed Wayne Gretzky approached the microphones, everyone suddenly knew why the press conference was called.

"The last three weeks have been a whirlwind for my wife and myself," said Gretzky, dabbing his eye to catch the tears that were falling. "But this was my own gut feeling and my own decision. I am disappointed in having to leave Edmonton," he said, holding back tears. "I promised 'Mess' [Mark Messier] I wouldn't do this."

Gretzky was traded to the Los Angeles Kings.

The next morning the city woke up to their morning papers' headlines blaring feelings of betrayal and deep sadness at the loss of their adopted hero. *The Edmonton Sun* chose to portray the city's mood with a headline that read "99 Tears." The entire nation was caught off-guard that the greatest hockey player ever to come out of Canada was going to play in the United States...and in Los Angeles of all places. Looking for someone to blame, eyes turned to Oilers' owner Peter Pocklington; it was rumoured that he had been shopping the superstar around to other teams. Pocklington promptly denied the allegations and attempted to put the spotlight back onto Gretzky.

"He's a great actor. I thought he pulled it off beautifully when he showed how upset he was, but he wants the big dream," Pocklington said to a *Los Angeles Times* reporter on the day of the deal. "All of a sudden, he figures, 'Gee, I'll go and conquer that market.' Not only that, but he'll conquer the United States."

Pocklington's position was clear, and he wanted to let the Edmonton fans know where he stood on the matter.

He said "If they think their king walked the streets of Edmonton without ever having a thought of moving, they are under a great delusion."

Regardless of who was to blame for the trade, nothing changed on the ice for the Great One. It wasn't the uniform; it wasn't the team; it was the love of competition that drove him to his next accomplishment.

The 1989–90 season, Gretzky's 11th season in the NHL, began with the anticipation of Gretzky breaking one of the most significant records of his career. He ended the 1988–89 season with 1837 points; just 13 points shy of matchig Gordie Howe's all-time points record of 1850 in 26 seasons of professional hockey. The accomplishment was astonishing. Gretzky reached Howe's record in under half the time, and Gretzky went on to set an all-time points record that will likely never be broken.

The moment came just six games into the new season when the Kings faced off against the Edmonton Oilers. The coincidence was not missed on those who witnessed the game.

Media writers from all across North America were present for the big game, even Mr. Hockey himself, Gordie Howe, showed up to witness the history-making moment. They didn't have to wait long. At 4:35 of the first period, Bernie Nicholls set up a goal for Gretzky's 1850th point, tying Gordie Howe's all-time point record. Suddenly, it became possible that Gretzky might break the record against his former team...on which he'd scored a majority of those points. But the Oilers were not going to let it happen without a fight.

"We tried our best not to let him break the record. We would never hear the end of it if he got that point against us," said long-time friend and Oilers teammate Kevin Lowe. "Don't believe that humble exterior. He loves to brag."

The moment came with just under a minute left in the third period, with the Los Angeles Kings down by one goal. With the Kings putting pressure on the Oilers defence deep in their own zone, a scramble was created in front of the net after a shot came in from the blue line. Oilers goaltender Bill Ranford stopped the initial shot, but it trickled wide to a waiting Gretzky who somehow managed to sneak away from the defence for one moment and put the rebound in the back of the net to tie the game and get his record-breaking 1851st point. To add insult to injury, Gretzky scored the winner in overtime. The Edmonton crowd, in a show of class, gave Gretzky a round of applause like he'd never left the team and still was breaking records as a proud member of the Oilers.

The last major record to fall was again a mark set by Gordie Howe. When the 1993–94 season began, Gretzky was just 37 goals away from beating the career goal record of 801. He tied the record against San José goaltender Artus Irbe on March 20, 1994. Three days later, the Kings were to play host to the Vancouver Canucks.

The Great Western Forum was packed and 16,005 fans eagerly awaited the moment when Gretzky would break one of the most important individual records in the NHL. The moment came late in the second period on a rush started by Kings left-winger Luc Robitaille and defenceman Marty McSorley followed by Gretzky. As Robitaille carried the puck through the neutral zone and over the Vancouver blue line, he dropped the puck to Gretzky who passed it to McSorley, breaking down on the right wing on a two on one. McSorley then passed the puck back to Gretzky, who had an open net in front of him.

"When I got the puck back, I saw the whole net," Gretzky said after the game. "I couldn't believe I saw it."

Canucks defenceman Gerald Diduck, who was covering McSorley, had the only chance of stopping the record goal.

"I almost got a whack at it, but he put it in," Diduck added. "Now I will be in the Hall of Fame forever." Not officially, but as part of the story of the goal.

Gretzky had the 802nd goal of his career and one of the most memorable in his life. The game was stopped, and a 10-minute ceremony to mark the occasion was held. NHL Commissioner Gary Bettman put it best when he said, "You have always been the Great One but tonight you are the greatest."

Wayne Gretzky finished his career with 894 goals and 1963 assists for a total of 2857 points. He did more than just break hockey records; he came to symbolize a game that we all love. He had no special advantages growing up. He played the game of hockey and life with the same opportunities that all Canadians have. He is the kid on a backyard rink, in the dead of winter, dreaming about making the National Hockey League.

Chapter Two

THE LAST LINE
...Defence

Bobby Orr
Offensive Defenceman

I t doesn't happen often that a single player comes along and changes the way the game is played.

There once was a time in the rules of hockey when goaltenders who fell to the ice to make a save were penalized two minutes. All that changed with Clint Benedict, goaltender for the Ottawa Senators. The problem was that Benedict always fell to the ice to make a save, and he was getting penalized several times in a game. Frustrated at having to give out so many penalties to the acrobatic goaltender, the league finally changed the rules to allow goaltenders to fall to the ice and make a save any way they saw fit.

Wayne Gretzky forced teams to rethink their defensive systems after he led the Oilers through the golden years of the '80s. During their reign in the 1980s, the Edmonton Oilers scored the most goals by a team in one season (446) in 1983–84. Oilers hold the number two, three, four and five spots on the list as well, and all were scored during those firewagon years of the 1980s.

Bobby Orr also changed the game as one of the first defencemen to bring an offensive strategy to the game. Defencemen always remained solid in their positions behind the forward line and rarely left the blue line to get a shot at the net. The defenceman was a reliable position player who made passes and held his zone against the other teams. If a defenceman managed to score 50 points in a season, he was considered a great asset to any team.

Bruins scouts got wind of a young defenceman who could defend his zone with the skill of Doug Harvey and could rush up the ice and score a goal in the style of Gordie Howe. During Bobby Orr's days with the Oshawa Generals of the Ontario Hockey Association, he was one of the most effective players on the ice. In his final year with the Generals, Bobby Orr recorded 38 goals and 56 assists in 47 games. His skills in the 1966 Memorial Cup final earned him a spot on the Bruins' roster; he made his professional debut later that year at the start of the 1966–67 NHL season.

Orr's impression on the league was immediate. He won the Calder Trophy for the league's best rookie and was named to his first of many All-Star games. He played excellent hockey in his first two seasons but wouldn't break out of his shell until the 1969–70 season.

While Orr was definitely not the first defence-man to rush into the offensive zone with the puck, he was the first to use his skills to such a devastating degree. Many teams were frustrated at his non-traditional approach to the defensive position and had a hard time containing him in one area of the rink. The Boston Garden crowd always held their breath just before the moment Orr broke out from behind the net and rushed to the other end untouched to score a goal or make a beautiful pass. By combining the rushing defensive talents of Orr with the solid offensive finishing touch of Phil Esposito, Boston Head Coach Harry Sinden created one of the most effective two-way teams in the NHL at the time. Orr ended the regular season with a record-breaking 120 points in one season, and he was the first-ever defenceman to win a scoring title. The line mates became so effective that the Bruins found themselves in the Stanley Cup finals with a three-game lead over the St. Louis Blues as game four headed into overtime.

The picture is one of the best reflections of what hockey is at its best. Every hockey fan has seen the picture of Bobby Orr flying through the air, arms high above his head in celebration after scoring the overtime goal to win the Stanley Cup. Even when it happened, it seemed like it was happening in slow motion.

Orr broke out in front of Blues goaltender Glenn Hall, hoping to get the puck by him. Blues defenceman Noel Picard was just a fraction too late, upending the Bruins defenceman after he put the puck in the net. Overcome at winning the Stanley Cup, Orr raised his arms in triumph as he fell through the air, seemingly unaware that the ice was quickly rushing up at him.

"I always tell Bobby he was up in the air for so long that I had time to shower and change before he hit the ice," said Glenn Hall, recalling the famous goal.

Next season Orr improved his season totals (despite the nagging knee injury that plagued him throughout his entire career) to collect the most points ever by a defenceman in one season with 139 total. The only defenceman to come close was Paul Coffee who ended the 1986 season with 138 points when he played for the Edmonton Oilers.

With each passing year, Orr's knees deteriorated to the point where he could no longer effectively play his position and score those end-to-end goals that made him famous in Boston. After just nine full seasons of professional hockey, Orr was forced to retire from the game he loved at the young age of 31. One can only guess what his career would have looked like if he had not been sidelined with the recurrent knee injuries. Nonetheless, he remains one of the best players to stand on the blue line.

Ray Bourque and Paul Coffey
In the Footsteps of Bobby Orr

Just as the great Bobby Orr announced his retirement, two young defencemen were making their mark in the minor leagues and were obviously watching how Orr played the game. Both possessed excellent defensive instincts as well as a signature skating and stickhandling ability that allowed them to move the puck like their mentor. Yet, each player brought their own talents to the position and left their marks in the NHL record books.

Raymond Bourque joined the NHL for his first season with the Boston Bruins in 1979. Possessing a bruising slapshot, Bourque was at home on the blue line and quickly made his impression on goaltenders of the league. In any scenario, the young defenceman performed his duties by the book. Bourque was never as aggressive as Orr was with the offensive manoeuvres, but he could get around an opposing player and find an open spot behind the goaltender with pinpoint accuracy. In only his first season, he put up respectable rookie numbers, played in his first All-Star game and finished the year off with the Calder Trophy as the top rookie in the National Hockey League. He went on to earn a selection in every All-Star game in his first 17 seasons, breaking the record previously held by Gordie Howe.

Bruins fans quickly grew attached to the young defenceman with steely eyes and a contagious smile. Bourque knew he had a lot to prove to the fans that had grown so attached to Bobby Orr. Orr brought the crowd excitement. He gave them something to cheer about, and he brought in two Stanley Cups. Bourque quickly got out from under Orr's shadow by scoring a career-high 96 points in the 1983–84 season. He also provided some the-atrics of his own on the ice that quickly made him a fan favourite. The one thing that was missing from his outstanding career was a Stanley Cup. He came closest with the Bruins in the 1988 Stanley Cup finals against the Edmonton Oilers.

The Bruins gained momentum after they defeated the Montréal Canadiens in the Adams division final. It was the first time in 18 playoff series (dating back to 1945) that the Bruins defeated the Canadiens. The Bruins later disposed of the New Jersey Devils on their way to the finals to meet the talent-filled Edmonton Oilers. Bourque fought hard on every shift, but the Oilers would not be held back, and by the third period of game four with the score tied 3–3, he knew he had only one more chance to turn the series around. But the gods of hockey were not so kind to the Bruins that year.

Late in the third as both teams pressed for the game-winning goal, a power failure at the Boston Gardens threw a blanket of darkness over the arena and immediately put a halt to the game. Players could barely see their way off the ice through the low emergency lights; the referees were forced to suspend the game to be played again another day. That incident did not work in Bourque's favour as the Oilers won the fifth game and took the Stanley Cup Championship. He wouldn't come that close to the Stanley Cup again until his final year in the National Hockey League.

Nearing the end of his hockey career, with the Stanley Cup still eluding him, Bourque asked to be traded to a cup-contending team and was dealt to the Colorado Avalanche on March 6, 2000. This was an emotional move for a veteran defenceman who played his entire career in a city that he called home for so many years. In a show of class, the Boston fans sent Bourque off to seek his cup with their blessing and with the comfort of knowing that he would always be remembered for what he accomplished as a member of the Bruins.

Along the way Bourque kept racking up points, and he ended his hockey days with three NHL regular season records for defencemen with 410 goals and 1169 assists for a total of 1579 points. After announcing that 2001 was going to be his last season, Bourque went into the playoffs knowing that this was his last shot at the coveted cup. He'd waited his entire career to hold the Stanley Cup above his head, and when the Colorado Avalanche beat the New Jersey Devils, team Captain Joe Sakic immediately handed the cup to Bourque. All his records considered, Bourque could count that as the best moment in his hockey career.

"I think it was a great story how everything came together in the end," said Bourque as he was being drenched with champagne by his fellow teammates. "I just thought it was a special story for hockey."

Paul Coffey began his career at the best time and with the best team to compliment his style. Led by Wayne Gretzky, the Oilers' brand of hockey was fast-paced with an accent on the offensive side of the game. Joining the league a year after Bourque, Coffey's style mirrored that of the young Bobby Orr. Coffey developed a knack for scoring early on; always jumping in on the rush with Gretzky, Messier or Kurri and more often than not coming out of it with a goal or an assist. He saw his point totals rise consistently over the next four years, registering three consecutive 100-plus point seasons. In the 1985–86 season, Coffey had the best season of his career with 138 points, just one shy of breaking Bobby Orr's season point record for a defenceman. Coffey did, however, set a regular season record when the defenceman scored the most goals at 48, beating Orr's total of 46. Coffey tied another record that year, equalling Tom Bladon's record for defencemen with 8 points in a single game.

After winning its third Stanley Cup, the Oilers dynasty slowly began to break up, with Coffey traded to the Pittsburgh Penguins in 1987. He remained a dominant offensive force with the Penguins teamed up with Mario Lemieux. Coffey won his last Stanley Cup with the Penguins in 1991. Winning the Stanley Cup seemed to be an omen for Coffey as he was traded the next season to the Los Angeles Kings. Although Coffey's numbers began to decline over the next few years it was not because he was no longer the player he was in the '80s. Rather, injuries limited the number of games he played for the rest of his career, but he continued to contribe to each of his teams. In 1995 he won the Norris Trophy while playing for the Detroit Red Wings, and he led the team in scoring with 90 points by the last game.

After being shopped around to several NHL teams, Coffey ended his career with the Boston Bruins at the top of the all-time defencemen scoring list, only to be eclipsed by Ray Bourque in 2001.

Despite all the teams he played for, Coffey will always be remembered as an Edmonton Oiler. It was there that he made his first mark on the NHL as a defenceman and where he would be most fondly remembered.

A space in the Hockey Hall of Fame is already reserved for the defensive legend.

Al Iafrate
Hardest Shot in the NHL

Since the slapshot became an important part of the game in the early 50s, players like Bernie "Boom Boom" Geoffrion and Bobby Hull have always kept goaltenders on their toes when they wound up to take a shot. As the years passed and players became bigger and stronger and the sticks became lighter and more flexible, the speed of the puck flying at the goaltenders has increased substantially.

The problem was that goaltenders couldn't give an accurate measurement of which player had the hardest shot. It wasn't until the implementation of the radar gun that the NHL had an accurate measurement of the hardest shot.

The NHL began measuring the hardest shots in the All-Star skills competition, which is held every year prior to the All-Star game. The player who currently holds the title is former Washington Capitals defenceman Al Iafrate. He set the record at a bruising 170 kilometres per hour in the 1993 All-Star skills competition.

Chapter Three

GOALTENDERS
Behind the Mask

Terry Sawchuk
Iron Man

To know what kind of goaltender Terry Sawchuk was, just look at the photo from the March 4, 1966 edition of *Life* magazine. On opening up the pages, the reader sees a mass of scar tissue strewn across the face of one of the most exciting goaltenders in NHL history. The picture tells the story of all the sticks, pucks and errant fists that found their way onto Sawchuk's face, resulting in more than 400 stitches in all. This picture says all there is to say about the type of person who guarded the nets night after night. Sawchuk played simply for the love of the game and nothing else.

When Sawchuk joined the Detroit Red Wings in the 1950–51 season, they got a solid goaltender with lightning reflexes and a strong determination to win hockey games. That season he won Rookie of the Year and was named to his first All-Star game. He finished the season with a 1.90 goals-against average and 12 shutouts. Things couldn't have been better for the rookie goaltender, and they would get even better in his second year with the Detroit Red Wings.

The Red Wings were the best team that season, with the Montréal Canadiens not too far behind in the standings. Terry Sawchuk was one of the major reasons that the Detroit Red Wings enjoyed such a good season. He was a solid goalie who was difficult to beat. Many nights, when the Red Wings were out-shot 2–1, it was Sawchuk who backed his team and often kept the other team off the scoreboard.

His talents really came to light in the 1951–52 playoffs. That year, Sawchuk posted a record that has not been broken to this day. A goalie can be the best there is during the regular season but if he can't perform in the playoffs, his accomplishments are more than likely forgotten. Lord Stanley has a way of proving the talent of players, and Sawchuk didn't waste any time.

In the playoff semi-finals, Sawchuk kept frustrating the Toronto Maple Leafs with a solid performance and many acrobatic saves to win the series in a four-game sweep. The Red Wings met their regular season rivals, the Montréal Canadiens, in the finals for the Stanley Cup championship.

The 1951–52 regular season ended with Detroit ahead of their division rivals, the Canadiens, by 12 points. Throughout the hockey season, whenever these two teams met it was guaranteed to be an emotional game. Throughout the late '40s and early '50s, Montréal and Detroit battled for the league title. Montréal would lose a heartbreaker to the Red Wings, and another time, Montréal would come away from the battle victorious.

Both teams played an open game and had the firepower to back it up. Red Wings player Gordie Howe was the leading scorer for his team, always posing a threat whenever he got the puck and caught his stride. The Canadiens' Maurice "the Rocket" Richard was unpredictable and talented. He could score on a goaltender in a hundred different ways, and he never chose the same way twice. Howe and Richard also had the devastating shooting ability of Bernie "Boom Boom" Geoffrion and the natural style of Jean Beliveau. Facing them down every night was Terry Sawchuk.

The series was hard fought on both sides, but the Canadiens just could not seem to put any shots behind Sawchuk, who posted four straight wins to take home the Stanley Cup. Sawchuk won eight straight games and kept his goals-against average to 0.62, which is a record playoff low. To this day, no one has broken the record. He won the Stanley Cup again in 1954 and 1955 with the Red Wings. In just five complete seasons, he recorded an incredible 57 shutouts.

Part of Sawchuk's success lay in the fact that players confronting him for the first time were not used to his style of play. Sawchuk crouched low to the ground and kept his arms to the sides and ready, whereas most goaltenders in that era played the game in a more upright position. His style allowed him to reach the shots that came in along the ice quicker than a stand-up goaltender could, and it increased his ability to move laterally and use his leg or glove for a quick grab. He played every game like it was the seventh game of the Stanley Cup finals. His intensity was legendary both on and off the ice. On the ice, Sawchuk was known to confront fans if they gave him a hard time, and he lost his temper at the slightest provocation. Even his teammates noticed that the man was different from the other players.

"Ukey's (Sawchuk's nickname) a strange bird," a fellow Red Wings teammate once said of him. "You can be joking with him one minute in the dressing room, and then you'll see him walking down the street later, and he'll walk right by you."

Goaltenders were a special breed in the original six teams of the National Hockey League. They were the heart and soul of any winning team. If your goaltender wasn't having a good season, it was almost impossible to be considered a contending team, since the talent pool of the original six league was filled with such great players. It was the era of star forwards and the star goalies hired to stop them, and Sawchuk was at the top of that list. Not all goaltenders had what it took to remain dominant in the original six. Teams in those days did not have back-up goaltenders, so it was left to one man to hold the fort. On many occasions, Sawchuk took a puck in the face and was carried off the ice to get stitched up, and he was expected to come out and play the remainder of the game.

With the constant pressure to perform and the intense determination that Sawchuk brought to every game, the stress finally got the better of him in the 1956–57 season. After posting a 2.00 goals-against average and taking his team all the way through to win the Stanley Cup, Sawchuk was traded to the Boston Bruins to make way for a young goaltender who was making noise in the minors—Glenn Hall. Sawchuk, initially unhappy with the trade, did not perform the way he had for the Red Wings and finally suffered a breakdown that forced him into an early retirement. After a lengthy recuperation, Sawchuk was traded back to the Red Wings in 1957. However, just two years later, the Stanley Cup championship team that Sawchuk had left was no longer the powerhouse that they used to be. Detroit now found itself fighting to stay out of the bottom of the league. Still, Sawchuk continued to produce reliable results. In the 1963–64 season, Sawchuk recorded his 95th shutout, surpassing the great George Hainsworth's all-time career shutout record of 94.

The league began to change in the '60s. Hockey became more of a science. Players started learning each other's habits on the ice, looking for strengths and weaknesses in all aspects of their opponents' game. It was also the time of Bobby Hull and his infamous curved stick slap shots. Goaltenders could no longer anticipate with certainty where a shot would go, as the curved sticks sent the puck in every direction. They became more vulnerable, and as a consequence Sawchuk could no longer produce the numbers he did early on in his career.

Before the start of the 1964 season, Sawchuk was traded in an inter-league draft that saw him moved to the Toronto Maple Leafs, where he was teamed with Johnny Bower. The two goaltenders were completely different from one another. Whereas Johnny Bower was one of the hardest working players on the team, attending all the practices and training sessions, Sawchuk put in very little effort in the practices.

Toronto Coach Punch Imlach asked Sawchuk why he didn't put any effort into stopping the puck during the practices, to which Sawchuk replied, "I figure I only have so many saves left in me, and I want to save them for the games."

It was in the 1966–67 season that Sawchuk hit his 100th career shutout mark, and along with Bower, he took the Toronto Maple Leafs to the Stanley Cup final and won their last Stanley Cup.

After this cup-winning season, Sawchuk was dealt to the Los Angeles Kings in the expansion draft, and after one mediocre season, he was traded back to his original team. Sawchuk was no longer the same goaltender he was in his early days. He seemed to be playing the game out of necessity rather than with the determination that fuelled him in his first few seasons. He ended his hockey career with the New York Rangers, playing only eight games during the season. But he managed to record a final shutout and established a career shutout record at 103.

Sawchuk played his last season after the Boston Bruins eliminated the New York Rangers from the 1970 playoffs. One night just after the series ended, Sawchuk and fellow Rangers roommate Ron Stewart were involved in an altercation. While it is not clear what happened, Sawchuk fell during the scuffle. He sustained internal injuries and was rushed to the hospital. Doctors tried for a month to stabilize his condition, but eventually, Sawchuk died from a blood clot in his lungs. Rangers Coach Emile Francis was at Sawchuk's bedside when he died and said: "To me, Sawchuk was probably the greatest goalie ever to play hockey."

Many years later people still say the same thing about the hot-blooded goaltender with a knack for keeping a little round rubber disc out of the net.

Patrick Roy
Inc-Roy-able!

The Montréal Canadiens drafted Patrick Roy, a skinny kid from Québec City, 51st overall in the 1984 draft. He was having a less-than-desirable record in his final year with the Granby Bisons of the Québec Major Junior Hockey League when he recorded a 5.55 goals-against average. Not exactly the numbers that Montréal Canadiens management would like to have seen, but they also saw something in the young man that they could work with and develop into the number-one goaltender on the team.

Just two years later, the rookie backstopped the Canadiens into the playoffs, where he made his mark on the National Hockey League. In the third game of the semi-final round of the 1986 playoffs between the Canadiens and the New York Rangers, Roy came into his own by stopping shot after shot, keeping the Canadiens alive and turning the series in the Canadiens' favour as they rode the wave of excitement in the Forum that night to a 4–3 win.

"The tension was overwhelming, and the fans were screaming 'Roouu-ah, Roouu-ah.' It got me off to a good start in the NHL," said Roy of his most memorable moment in hockey.

The Canadiens went on to defeat the Rangers and eventually win the cup while riding the success of the rookie goaltender. Roy won the Conn

Smythe Trophy as the most valuable player in the playoffs, keeping his goals-against average to a low 1.92 and enjoying a .923 save percentage.

It wasn't just the numbers that made him an instant fans' favourite. He was also fun to watch.

Fans stared curiously at the young goaltender who collected a few strange mannerisms over time, as many goaltenders tend to do. He would constantly shake his head from side to side as if his helmet didn't fit him. Another favourite was before a face-off, he skated to both corners of his net and bent down to seemingly talk to his goal posts. Although, what the fans really enjoyed was his perfecting of the butterfly style. Facing the shooter squarely, Roy opened up his five-hole only to take it away at the last second by dropping to his knees in what is called the butterfly position. Many star forwards fell victim to the apparently easy goal, only to have it taken away at the snap of Roy's pads. Banners quickly sprouted up in and around the Montréal Forum: "Inc-Roy-Able!" (Incredible).

Roy got another chance to hoist the Stanley Cup over his head in the 1989 playoff finals, when the Canadiens took on the Calgary Flames. Although history was not to repeat itself, Roy led the way with brilliant goaltending that kept the underdog Canadiens alive through each hard-fought series. Roy secured himself a position among the top goaltenders in the NHL over the years and would eventually win another Stanley Cup in the 1993 playoffs.

Going into the 1993 playoffs, Canadiens fans had little hope of winning the Stanley Cup that year. They had a good team, but their star goaltender played a surprisingly terrible season, posting his worst goals-against average since his rookie season. But the measure of a professional goaltender and athlete is one that can perform in the playoffs when the pressure and the risks are at their peak. Once again, Patrick made the difference through the Canadiens' playoff run. After falling behind to the Québec Nordiques in the first round, two games to none, Roy's fortune quickly turned around. He finished the post-season with a 16–4 record with 10 consecutive overtime victories. His name was once again engraved on the Conn Smythe Trophy and the Stanley Cup.

His fortunes with the Canadiens, however, were running out. After the Canadiens failed to make the playoffs in 1995, Roy received most of the attention from the media, blaming him for the failing fortunes of the team. When the Canadiens management brought on former Canadiens Mario Tremblay as head coach, Roy's days with the Canadiens came to an end.

Rumours circulated in the press that Tremblay and Roy were not getting along behind the scenes. Everything came to a head on the night when the Detroit Red Wings rolled into town. After he let in a few easy goals, the Montréal crowd started to taunt Roy every time he made a save. Tremblay finally decided to pull Roy after he let in nine goals. This was the last straw in an already-strained relationship with the Canadiens upper management. On leaving the ice, Roy removed his helmet and walked over to his team's president and told him he'd just played his last game in a Canadiens uniform. Roy was eventually traded to the Colorado Avalanche, where he continued to be one of the top goaltenders in the league.

After years of piling up win after win, Roy finally reached the career wins record set by Hall of Fame goaltender Terry Sawchuk at 447 wins. The moment came when the Colorado Avalanche defeated the Washington Capitals in a 4–3 overtime victory. Several days later, before a game between the Avalanche and the Florida Panthers, National Hockey League President Gary Bettman gave a speech in honour of Roy's achievement in a 25-minute ceremony before the start of the game.

"Roy's feat isn't something you can accomplish by having a good season," said Bettman that day. "This is something you only accomplish by having years of good seasons, over a lifetime of playing. When you also take into account that he did it in 121 fewer games than Terry Sawchuk, to say he has had a truly outstanding career doesn't say it well enough."

Roy finished his career with a record-establishing 551 regular season wins in 1029 games and a play-off record of 151 wins; numbers that are not likely to be broken for some time.

Ken McAuley, Sam LoPresti,
or Ron Tugnutt?
Most Shots on Goal

Who was the goaltender to face the most shots in an NHL game? The question remains open to debate. Prior to 1955, certified statistics were not kept on how many shots on goal were taken during a game. Often "shots on goal" meant whenever a shot was taken in the direction of the net. This meant any time a shot was deflected or just missed it was often noted as an actual "shot." Instead of the average 26–35 shots per game, shots on net were often recorded at around 35–50.

In a game that took place on February 19, 1944, between the Montréal Canadiens and the New York Rangers, Rangers goaltender Ken McAuley faced 91 shots in total. He stopped 86 to lose the game 5–3. Strangely enough, Ken McAuley backstopped the Rangers in another game against the Red Wings and gave up 15 goals in the most lopsided victory in National Hockey League history. After registering an abysmal 6.20 goals-against average that season, McAuley was sent back to the minor leagues, and he never again found his way back into the NHL.

Another possibility for the shots on goal record came three years earlier in a game between the Chicago Blackhawks and the Boston Bruins in March 1941. The Bruins fired 83 shots on Chicago goaltender Sam LoPresti, who managed to stop 80 of them. His incredible efforts did not pay off, however, as the Bruins won the game 3–2. After one year in the military, LoPresti never again played another game in the NHL.

Ron Tugnutt, playing for the Québec Nordiques at the time, holds the modern-day record for the most shots on goal when he faced the Boston Bruins in March 1991. Tugnutt's bid for the record would turn out to be better than McAuley or LoPresti. Tugnutt stopped 70 out of 73 shots to end up in a 3–3 tie. As to who exactly holds the record, well, maybe they all can share it.

Manon Rheaume
A Moment in the Big Leagues

She was always at the top of her game. During her time with the Canadian Women's National Team she backstopped them to numerous title championships and came close to winning an Olympic gold in 1998. She has an aggressive outlook on the game and is always looking for new challenges when it comes to improving how she plays.

Goaltenders have always been known as the odd personality on the team. It is a position that does not have room for someone who hesitates or who second-guesses themselves. Decisions must be made in a split second. Rheaume already proved successful in women's hockey and set her sights on breaking into the one place remaining for her to challenge herself. After a summer of intensive training and mental preparation, Rheaume earned a highly coveted spot in the Tampa Bay Lightning training camp in fall of 1992.

Some criticized General Manager Phil Esposito's signing of Rheaume as a publicity stunt. The team had just entered the NHL the previous year and could have used the attention with all the other professional sports in the region fighting for spectators. Regardless of the motives, Rheaume became the first woman to play in a National Hockey League game. Her début came during a pre-season game against the St. Louis Blues. In the 20 minutes she played, Rheaume made seven saves on nine shots. Jeff Brown scored on a shot from the point, and Brendan Shanahan potted the other on a one-timer that beat the rookie goaltender. Rheaume played a solid game and made an immediate impression on those who saw her make history that night. She was signed that year to the Lightning's farm team but never made it back into the NHL to play another game. For the goaltender who always wanted to go higher in her career, she made it to the top...even if it was only for 20 minutes.

Chapter Four

CANADA'S BEST
on the International Stage

The Summit Series 1972:
Canada versus the USSR
Hockey Unites a Nation

The series remained tied after a long, hard-fought battle between Canada and the USSR. With just under two minutes remaining, Canada pressed the Russians. Foster Hewitt called the game for the listeners across Canada who were glued to their radios and television sets.

The Canadian team went into a huddle there, which seems to be a little unusual. [Word lost] ...they're really fighting. The puck comes up at centre ice. Vasiliev carries it back into his zone, to Shadrin who missed it. Peter Mahovlich is at centre, driving it into the Soviet zone. Liapkin gets there first. Cournoyer just touched it. Savard, getting it at centre ice, clearing it off a skate. It goes into the Canadian zone. Yakushev, a dangerous player, is belted on that play. Cournoyer rolled it out, Vasiliev going back to get it. There's 1:02 left in the game.

A cleared pass on the far side. Liapkin rolled one to Savard. Savard clears a pass to Stapleton. He cleared the open wing to Cournoyer. Here's a shot! Henderson made a wild stab for it and fell. Here's another shot, right in front...They score! Henderson scores for Canada! And the fans and the team are going wild! Henderson, right in front of the Soviet goal with 34 seconds left in the game!

Canadians always thought of themselves as the best hockey players in the world. To Canadians, it was a given that Canada was the best on the ice. But in the frozen land of Soviet Russia, a team was making inroads into the Canadians' title as world hockey champions. The Soviets won several world championships and walked away from the Winter Olympics with gold. When the opportunity came along to have the NHL's finest take on the "amateur" talent of the Soviet Union, the media quickly predicted that the eight-game series would end in a sweep in favour of the talent-filled Canadian roster. The professionals of Canadian hockey could not lose against a team of unknown communists. The Soviets were from a different world and could not beat Canada's finest at their very own game. The country quickly awoke to the possibility that Canada might not own its hockey bragging rights.

The Montréal Forum played host for the first game as the long-anticipated series was set to start. The game even drew both countries' best politicians, with the Soviet ambassador and Canadian Prime Minister Pierre Elliot Trudeau in attendance for the ceremonial face-off. The Canadians came out on the ice to a great round of applause and the confidence of their country's people that they could defeat the unknowns. In their red CCCP jerseys the Soviet team took the ice a little overwhelmed at the task ahead of them.

"Before that first game we had a very nervous feeling," recalled Soviet player Boris Mikhailov. "It was scary. We just wanted to begin playing."

Their nerves showed early. Phil Esposito scored only 30 seconds into the game, and across Canada, the country went wild, now assured that winning was an easy task. Just a few minutes later, Paul Henderson scored on a slapshot from the top of the circle to make the game 2–0. Canadians eased back into their comfortable sofa chairs certain that the series was a *fait-accompli*.

But, everyone sat up quickly when the Soviets shook off their nervous jitters and quickly tied the game. The second period finished with the game under their control. Team Canada made a serious error in judging the talent that made up the Soviet squad.

In the dressing room, the turnaround in the game provided Team Canada with some time to brood over the fact that they had seriously mis-judged the talent of the Soviets.

"At that point, there was an absolutely sicken-ing feeling," recalled Henderson. "We all knew that the sleeping giant had been awoken and we were going to have a fight on our hands."

From then on the game was a complete disaster from a Canadian standpoint. The Soviet players dominated the game on every level. This domina-tion continued in the second and third periods, and the Soviets went on to hand the Canadians an embarrassing 7–3 loss.

Team Canada was out-skated, out-hustled and constantly frustrated by the Soviet team and the dashing acrobatic talents of young Soviet goal-tender Vladislav Tretiak. Maybe it was that Team Canada had only practiced together for two weeks, and the Soviets had been playing together for a long time. Whatever the excuses, the result was still the same, and for the next game in Toronto the pressure was on for Team Canada to respond to the challenge that was now laid before them. After all, they were professionals.

Before game two at Maple Leaf Gardens, Coach Harry Sinden gathered his team around in the dressing room and addressed his downtrodden men. With the passion of a preacher, Sinden tried his best to restore the faith and conviction that was in such abundance before the start of the series.

The Canadians came out aggressively hounding the Soviet puck carriers, trying to force them into a play or to fall back and have to constantly regroup thereby slowing them down. It seemed to work as the Canadians were up 1–0 at the end of two periods. In the third period, the Canadians were controlling the game, and goaltender Tony Esposito was providing reliable watch over the net. The forwards responded with goals when they were called for. The game-breaker for the Canadians came, however, when Peter Mahovlich scored one of the nicest goals of the tournament.

After grabbing the puck in the neutral zone, the centre broke through the Soviet blue line and completely undressed Tretiak for a goal that sent the entire Canadian bench out on the ice to swarm over Mahovlich. The game ended with Canada winning 4–1 over the Soviet Union with game 3 set to take place in Winnipeg. The team had regained some confidence, and this time they were not going to let it get the best of them.

September 6, 1972. Game three. The series tied 1–1 and renewed hope before the players hit the ice in front of a rowdy crowd at the Winnipeg arena. Team Canada approached the game with the same strategy as before—stay close to the guy with the puck, fore-check relentlessly and never fall asleep on the man-to-man coverage because the speed of the Soviet forwards could break at a moment's notice for odd-man rushes. Canada managed an early lead with goals by Jean-Paul Parise, Phil

Esposito and Jean Ratelle. But the Russians shook off the hard fore-checking of Team Canada and ended the game in a 4–4 tie. The young Soviet goaltender turned out another game-saving performance; the Soviets were out-shot 38–25.

Speaking after the game with head hunched down and a towel around his neck, Yvon Cournoyer leaned forward into the microphone. "We got ahead, let a lead slip away, but that just drove the point home again," he said, wiping the dripping sweat off his forehead. "No matter if we were on a power play or playing even strength, the Russians were always dangerous. Sometimes, though, it just takes awhile to sink in."

Even though the game ended in a tie, it felt like the Canadians had lost and dissention quickly started to tear away at the team.

"We were having problems on the ice; some guys were complaining about not playing; and we always seemed to have a different lineup each game," said Cournoyer. "It just never seemed to work as well as it could."

The emotions were reaching a climax in the Team Canada camp as the media began to question the abilities of the team, and the fickle public's confidence began to wane. It seemed very likely that Canada was about to lose its title as home of the best hockey players in the world. All the doubts, rumours and frustrations seemed to come to a head when the series pulled into its fourth and final stop of the Canadian leg of the tournament—in Vancouver at the Pacific Coliseum.

The media had the public up in arms over the embarrassing way in which the Russians were beating the Canadians at their own game. Coach Harry Sinden was always second-guessed on every decision he made. When he put in Dryden for the fourth game (after his horrible performance in the 7–3 loss in Montréal) instead of Tony Esposito (who kept the Canadians in the series after some key saves), the discontent was palpable in the arena as the teams took to the ice.

In just over a minute after the first face-off, the crowd turned on the first Canadian player to show any sign of weakness. Team Canada was caught off-guard by the chilly reception that the 15,000-plus fans at the Pacific Coliseum had waiting for them. The Soviets took advantage of the mood, quickly going up 2–0 by the end of the first period.

"It was obvious that the fans weren't completely with us in this one," said backup goaltender Eddie Johnston between the first and second periods. And the taunting from the crowd only escalated as the game wore on.

About halfway through the third period, Soviet forward Vladimir Shadrin put his team up by two goals and effectively took the Canadian players and whatever fans that were left out of the game. Team Canada added one goal, but the Russians had the game sealed and ended up winning 5–3 over a crushed Canadian team and an even more disappointed crowd that booed their team relentlessly. The fans were let down by their country's best, and they felt it was their right to vent their anger.

Yvon Cournoyer added after the game: "I really think the people of Vancouver forgot that this still was a hockey game. But I guess it had become more than that. But the people were also wrong to boo us. It's not like we went there to lose."

After the game as the players slowly skated off the ice with their tails between their legs, Phil Esposito walked over to a CBC reporter with the intent of letting the Canadian public know how all the bad press and booing was tearing apart the Canadian team.

Upset and clearly emotionally overcome, Esposito delivered a straight-from-the-heart response to all the criticism that was laid on the team.

"To the people across Canada, we're trying our best. The people boo us. We're all disappointed, disenchanted. I can't believe people are booing us," said an impassioned Esposito, staring directly into the CBC camera. "Let's face facts. They've got a good team. We're all here because we love Canada. It's our home, and that's the only reason we came."

The rallying cry was sent out. If Canada wouldn't support their team, then the team was going to have to win the series for itself. Team Canada had two exhibition games in Sweden to help them acclimatize to the different style of hockey played by Europeans before continuing on to the series in Moscow. The stop in Sweden was a welcome distraction from the negative media attention Team Canada was receiving for its performances against the Soviets. The players were able to work on their team play while at the same time becoming used to the larger ice surface, the pace of a European game and the Swedish players' dirty stick work.

The mood in the Canadian camp began to shift; their system began to gel; and they came together as a group. Although they were not the most pleasant games to watch, Sweden provided the players with the proper atmosphere to bring this group of NHL stars together as a team. Facing the possibility of an embarrassing series defeat, the team unified under the intense media scrutiny and public pressure. They left Sweden for Moscow with a renewed sense of hope and the feeling that they could win the series if they played as a team.

"When we went over there, it seemed like everyone was against us," said forward J.P Parise. "I think that brought us all a lot closer as a team."

After getting off the plane, the Canadian players arrived in a different world like nothing anyone on the team experienced before. This was the land of communist Russia. The Iron Curtain had been up for so long that outsiders knew little of the daily life of most Russian people. Moscow was in the midst of a gloomy September as the players got their first look around the city. Everything was different. No Coca-Cola, no steak and the toilet paper left much to be desired. Luckily, some items were flown in to make the players feel less homesick and help them focus on the matter at hand—figuring out how to defeat a Soviet hockey team that dominated every aspect of the game.

The Canadians approached their next game with a more positive attitude. Regardless of all they had been through, they honestly thought they could beat the Soviet team on their home ice. Before the melancholy crowd of Russian fans, the Canadians took to the ice to the sound of loud cheers coming from the 2700 Canadian fans who had made their way to Moscow to support their team. It was almost impossible not to notice their presence at the game as their trumpets blared, and they began to chant "Da Da, Ca-na-da. Nyet Nyet, So-vi-et."

The game got underway, and Team Canada came out hard, fore-checking aggressively and not letting up on the Soviet forwards. The system paid off, and Team Canada was up 3–0 by the end of the second period. The Canadian contingent in the crowd was going wild, while the Russian fans remained stone-faced, only breaking the silence when the referee made a call they didn't like. At the start of the third, the Canadian players were back on their heels fighting to maintain their lead, but the Russian players came back with several quick goals to tie and eventually win the game by a score of 5–4.

Team Canada was despondent. They had let the Soviets back into the game again. After putting up a 4–1 lead in the third period, they made the same mistakes by letting the Soviets take control.

In just under six minutes, the Soviets scored four unanswered goals to win game five and put a stranglehold on the series, now at 3–1–1.

Paul Henderson described the mood of the players after the fifth game: "Never did anyone say after that game, 'Well, that's it, we're done.' We always had that feeling we were going to win. It sounds strange, but I never felt we were going to lose the series, not even after that game."

On the Soviet side of the series, things were looking pretty positive as the players now believed they could beat the Canadians at their own game. Russia had the Canadians on edge; they figured out how to beat them. The Canadians were demoralized and humiliated, and now all that was left was to put the series away with just one more win. The Soviets were riding high with confidence, and they began making the same mistake the Canadians had in the first four games of the series—they found a way to beat the Canadians and stuck to that game plan. Canada turned this around by continuing to deal with the walls thrown up by the Soviets.

It was do-or-die time for the Canadian team, and they knew it all too well. The atmosphere in the dressing room had a concerned positivity. They all knew what had to be done, and they were confident they could do it, but the Soviets were an excellent team that had been underestimated before. And, as the Soviets proved in game four, the game could turn to their favour in minutes.

For the sixth game, Coach Sinden put Dryden back in the net, giving Esposito a rest for a potential game seven start. As game six got underway, the Canadians quickly became aware that they were playing a European game with European officials who did everything in their power to slow them down. During the first period, the Canadians had to kill three minor penalties that never would have been called in the NHL. They came out of the first period with the score at 0–0, but Team Canada was fuming over the poor officiating, and it would only get worse.

With the game at 3–2 for Team Canada in the third period, Ron Ellis was given a questionable penalty with just under three minutes remaining. The Russians had a few chances, but Dryden and his team held them off to come away with a hard-fought victory. After the game, Bobby Orr waited in the wings for the referees to come off the ice, and he gave them a piece of his mind for their officiating. The Canadians won, but it took a toll on the players. The series became a bitter battle; it was a war on ice, and game seven was no different.

Game seven saw the Canadians come out flying. They potted the first goal just four minutes into the game, on a slapshot from the point by Ron Ellis that easily beat the normally solid Tretiak. The tenacious Russians came back, however, with two goals before the end of the period that put pressure on the Canadian squad. By the third period the game was deadlocked, and any battling along the boards began to get dirty. One incident had defenceman Gary Bergman and Soviet centre Boris Mikhailov fighting viciously behind the net for the puck; this cleared both benches. A brawl didn't break out, but all who were watching the game at the Russian arena could feel the bad blood between the two teams. When the game continued, the puck fell to Paul Henderson to get the game-winning goal.

It all happened so quickly. Bobby Clark won the face-off in the Canadian zone and managed to push the puck back to defenceman Guy Lapointe. The Canadian fans in the crowd began to chant again. Lapointe spotted NHL teammate Serge Savard behind the net and shot a pass directly to the tape of his stick. Looking up to find a path out of his own zone, Savard caught sight of Henderson quickly making his way through to the neutral zone. Savard passed to Henderson. Henderson then had two Russian defencemen to contend with before getting clear for a chance at Tretiak. He rushed the two defencemen, trying to stick handle the puck around them.

Tretiak saw him coming. He crouched down, set his stick down solid on the ice, brought his glove up and stared at the streaking Henderson.

Henderson tried to skirt around the Russian defencemen, but one hit him hard enough that Henderson went down. Not giving up, Henderson somehow managed to get the puck through the defenceman's legs and get off a shot that beat a sur-prised Tretiak by going underneath his arm for the game-winning goal. Henderson did it again. Even the normally subdued Russian fans appreciated the effort of the Canadian forward. Team Canada poured onto the ice and surrounded their game hero. The Russians slowly slid off the ice, knowing that they might have lost control of the series.

September 28, 1972. The drama began even before the puck was dropped. The Canadian camp learned early on that the same officials that handed Canada over 30 minutes in penalties and Russia only four were going to be at the final game of the deadlocked series. The Russians could smell defeat and were doing everything in their power to beat the renewed Canadian squad. The Canadian camp was angry at the referee change but somehow not surprised at the underhanded tactics on the Soviets' part. Both teams finally agreed on two referees, and the series continued.

They were about to play the game of their careers. It became more than just a mere hockey game. After all that the Canadians had been through, it was less about winning a game and more about winning a war. Two ways of life, two ways of playing the game, and one had to come out of the series as the reigning champions of the hockey world. These were the best from both countries, and they were playing for keeps.

The final game. Canada watched and listened with a renewed sense of hope after they saw their weary team battle back in the series. But as soon as the puck was dropped, the Canadians found themselves once again packed tight in the penalty box with two men down. The Russian power play was too strong for the penalty killers as winger Alexander Yakushev put in a rebound past a sprawled-out Dryden. The bad calls didn't end there. J.P. Parise was given an interference penalty for checking a Russian player outside of the play. Parise had enough of these calls. He charged Referee Kompalla and pretended to knock him over the head with his stick, earning himself a game misconduct. The Canadian bench littered the ice in protest of the flagrantly biased calls.

The players of Team Canada held in their rage and continued with the job at hand. When a Soviet defenceman was sent to the penalty box for two minutes, Team Canada took the opportunity and evened the score with a goal from Phil Esposito at 6:45 of the first period. After another Soviet goal, Canada tied the score 2–2 before the end of the first period.

The Team Canada dressing room was electric after the first period. They stuck to their game, and the Russians were fighting to keep up despite the continued bad calls from the referees.

Sinden quickly got the attention of the players. "Good effort, guys. That's the kinda game I like to see out there. Anything can happen out there at a moment's notice, but I haven't seen any of you stumble. We know we can beat these guys. Now go out there and show them that Canada owns this game." And in a clamour of sticks and shouts, they went back out on the ice for the second period.

The back-and-forth battle continued as Russia pulled ahead, quickly followed by another equalizing Canadian goal. But relentless pressure by the Soviet forwards broke down the Canadian defences, and Russia scored two more goals to put them up 5–3 by the end of the second period. Canada tried nearly everything to put a goal behind Tretiak, but the Russian goalie was having a typically spectacular game.

Team Canada knew this was their time. The dressing room was unusually quiet. The players felt no need to talk about what they had to do; each one of them knew their job. They were anxious to get back out on the ice. This was their series to win. This was their game.

The Russians could feel the game slipping away just a few minutes into the third period. The puck was deep in the Russian zone. Mahovlich battled in the corner for control of the puck. He came out with the puck on his stick and caught Esposito in front of the net with a pass that he knocked out of the air to put in right behind Tretiak. Now they were just one point behind. The small Canadian contingent began to taunt the increasingly silent Soviet fans: "Da Da, Canada! Nyet Nyet, Soviet!"

Hoping to inspire his team and get back into the game, Russian Evgeny Mishakov picked the first fight of the series with Rod Gilbert. With a swift punch to the mouth of Mishakov, Gilbert gave Canada the final momentum it needed to take over the game. It wasn't long before Cournoyer topped Tretiak, tapping a rebound past the goalie and tying the game at five apiece.

Six minutes remaining. Canada could not afford to tie the game. If that happened, the Russians would win the game on the basis of a higher goal differential. Five minutes remaining. Back and fourth, both teams had their chances but neither Dryden nor Tretiak were going to let one get by without a fight. Four minutes left. Both Russian and Canadian fans were on the edges of their seats, knowing that they were watching one of the most competitive hockey games ever. Three, two, one minute remaining. Henderson called out to Mahovlich to get off the ice so that he could get on for the last shift. Henderson knew that if he could just get out there, he would be able to get one chance on Tretiak.

The Canadians shot the puck into the Soviet zone and pressed the defenceman, forcing him to make a pass that he would regret. Cournoyer caught the clearing attempt at the blue line. He tried to pass to Henderson, but the puck fell behind him and he went crashing into the boards. Esposito picked up the loose puck and tried to snap it past the goaltender, but Tretiak kicked out his leg to make the save. Henderson just moved out from the corner, and he caught sight of the puck near the sprawled-out goaltender and jammed at it. Tretiak stopped the first shot but left another rebound that Henderson quickly lifted over the Soviet goaltender for the game-winning goal.

After all the media scrutiny, the harsh treatment by Canadian fans in Vancouver, the demoralizing comeback wins by the Soviets...Canada won the series and reclaimed the title of best hockey team in the world. The images are unforgettable.

"Henderson has scored for Canada...."

Women's International Hockey
Canada's Golden Girls

Until the 1990s, women's hockey existed in the shadows of the more popular and well-funded men's hockey programs. When the first official Women's World Championship was to take place, every country involved scrambled to put together some semblance of a team. The problem was that no system existed to rank or evaluate individual players and put them together into a training camp. Coaches had to be hired, players needed to be evaluated and money needed to be channelled to the right areas if Canada was going to be a contender in women's international hockey. When the first championship came about in 1990, the Canadian team was disorganized enough to almost not allow Angela James—lauded as Canada's best female hockey player—into the tournament. The error was eventually corrected, and James signed on.

After donning on their bright, fluorescent pink uniforms, the Canadian women's team did not get much press or attention for the games that were held in Ottawa. If it weren't for the families and friends of the players, the atmosphere in the arena would have seemed like a local peewee championship rather than an international event.

Uniforms aside, the tournament was a complete success for the Canadian team. Despite the poor organization and lack of media attention, the Canadian women dominated the tournament to win all five of their games, scoring 61 and only allowing 8 goals against. Canada began its heated rivalry with the United States women's team in the final game for the gold medal, handing the U.S. a 5–2 defeat and taking the gold for Canada. The tournament not only proved that the Canadian women's team was the best in the world, but that Canada had a large enough pool of talent to put together a championship team.

Canada won again in 1992, and by 1994, the tournament was receiving attention from media and fans alike. The Canadian Hockey Association became involved behind the scenes, organizing events everywhere to raise awareness of women's hockey in Canada. These tournaments enabled coaches and managers for the World Championships to get a look at the talented players across Canada, who might have remained isolated in their communities. Jayna Hefford, one of Canada's now-veteran players, was discovered when she caught everyone's attention as one of the top scorers in the under-18 event and the 1995 Canada Winter Games.

As the uniforms improved, so did Team Canada, and they won again in 1994, 1997, 1999, 2000 and 2004. But as Team Canada improved, so did all the other teams that participated in the tournament. The rivalry between Canada and the United States heated up as the two teams met year after year to battle it out on-ice for the gold medal, and more importantly, bragging rights.

The year 1997 was a turning point for women's hockey. The International Olympic Committee announced that women's hockey was going to be a medal sport in the upcoming 1998 Olympic Winter Games in Nagano, Japan. Also, the 1997 World Championships were an enormous success with the public and especially the sports media. Players now had special training regimens, coaches and all the things they needed as money began to flow into the sport. They were getting faster and stronger, and the coaches started getting to know the other teams' strengths and weaknesses. Once again it was Canada and the United States in final for the gold. This time, however, it wasn't an easy run for the Canadians; it took an overtime goal by forward Nancy Drolet to defeat the U.S. 4–3 for the gold medal.

The United States would get revenge in the 1998 Olympics by winning the gold medal against the Canadians. It was a hard-fought game that had the Canadians down by a goal with a few minutes remaining, only to have an empty-net goal dash their hopes of winning the first Olympic medal given to the sport of women's hockey. The emotion of the moment overcame the Canadian team, who felt the hopes of their country on their shoulders.

"At first, you feel disbelief," said Canadian captain Stacy Wilson. "You have a dream for so many years. and all of a sudden it's over. Then, the thoughts go through your head of your family and friends and all of Canada...and thoughts lead to feelings. You see the medal and it's silver—feelings kick in pretty quick."

But Canada came back to win its sixth straight World Championship gold in 1999, and in 2002 they took the Olympic title away from the Americans by winning the gold medal in dramatic form, coming from behind to take back the bragging rights. It was Canada's game again.

Women's hockey has come a long way since the first official tournament in 1990, but the game is still evolving. Canada's 2000 Women's National Team Head Coach Melody Davidson put the future in perspective:

> *While demands on the national team players and coaches for training and competition are increasing, opportunities to earn a living at the game they love, and have devoted their lives to, aren't increasing at the same rate.*

Despite the obstacles, the future of women's hockey looks bright.

Hayley Wickenheiser
The Professional

In a CBC interview in 1994, 15-year-old Hayley
Wickenheiser talked about her talents as a hockey
player, the "female Wayne Gretzky" comparisons
and the possibility of one day maybe playing in a
men's professional league.

The 15-year-old responded aptly to the reporter's
questions, saying: "I guess I would want to do that,
but I don't know if it would be realistic. The size
and the strength differences are so incredible that
it's pretty tough to do."

At fifteen, Hayley Wickenheiser was too young
and too small to be playing against men in a full-
contact game. She needed to refine certain aspects
of her game to be able to play on a competitive
level with a men's team. The Women's National
Team provided the perfect training ground for
the young hockey star to sharpen her talents. At
her young age she was already a member of the
Women's World Championship team and as each
year went by, Hayley's skills as a hockey player
improved. But the obvious physical difference
between men and women would be something
that she could never overcome.

"I will never be able to play like the guys do. So
I just had to rethink my game," Hayley added.
"I prefer to use brains over brawn. It's like Gretzky
when he was younger, he was always too small to

play the physical game, so he adapted and made his own style to get around that."

The strategy worked for Wickenheiser. She continued to put up impressive numbers on the Women's National Team and was always considered a dominant figure on the ice, never afraid to lead with her body. The peak of her career with the Women's National Team came when Wickenheiser and her teammates dethroned the Americans to take the gold medal in the 2002 Olympic Winter Games in Salt Lake City. Riding high right after the gold medal victory, Wickenheiser needed another challenge. She climbed to the top in women's professional hockey with five World Championship titles and just added an Olympic gold medal to her collection.

"I looked at the Olympic gold in my hand and knew that I had gone as far as I could in women's hockey. The only place left where I still had something to prove to myself and to people around me was in a men's professional league."

Hayley wasted no time in vaulting the next hurdle. At the end of 2002, Hayley travelled to Europe where she quickly found a spot on a professional men's league in Finland, playing for Kirkkonummi Salamat.

It took a while for Wickenheiser to adjust to playing the game at a different speed, but she soon found her role on the team and began to make contributions to the team's success. Every week the news reported on the Canadian woman playing in a men's league, waiting for that moment when she got her first point. Some said that a woman should not be playing in a men's league, that she might get severely hurt when checked and that she cannot keep up with the pace of a man's game. Granted, she was not the greatest player on the team, but she made her contribution by playing a defensive-style game; she preferred to start plays rather than finish them off. Wickenheiser finally got her first point when she assisted on a goal in January 2003 thereby becoming the world's first woman to register a point in a professional men's game.

Wickenheiser surpassed a barrier that no other woman had done before. She brought much-needed attention to the sport of women's hockey, opening up the reality for future players that an athlete is not bound by gender to a certain sport. Hopefully, her accomplishments will encourage more girls to strap on the skates and play hockey.

Chapter Five

RIOTS, PLAGUES AND
Other Odd Hockey Moments

The Richard Riot

M arch 13, 1955. The Montréal Canadiens were taking on their rivals the Boston Bruins. At that point in the season, Richard was leading the league in scoring and was desperately trying to win his first scoring title ever, a mark that had eluded him for 10 years. In second and third place, right behind Richard, were teammates Bernie "Boom Boom" Geoffrion and Jean Beliveau.

The Canadiens had just come off a rough match with the Bruins at the Montréal Forum where Boston pounded Maurice heavily. It was not uncommon for opposing players to try and goad Richard into fights by any means possible. Often the choice method of some players was to make fun of his French heritage with words such as, "Frog!" and "French Bastard!"

Needless to say, Richard was not in the best of spirits for the Sunday night match at the Boston Gardens. He was bruised, battered and tired. When your team is at the top, opposition teams will try their best to defeat you in every way possible, and it was no different on this night at the Gardens.

"On this particular night, the Bruins were really up for us. They laid on the lumber at every opportunity, and by the time the game had reached the end of the first period, we were a very bruised bunch of men," noted Richard as he looked back to the moments that led to the riot.

That night, Boston defenceman Hal Laycoe was paying particular attention to keeping Richard tied up and frustrated. Laycoe, one of the few men in professional hockey to wear glasses, had broken into the league with the Rangers and moved around to a few teams before finally ending up with the Bruins. He wasn't known as a dirty player, but when the chance arose he wasn't known as the cleanest player either.

Physical and verbal jousting between Laycoe and Richard started early in the game. On one play, the Rocket was just about to skate around the big defenceman with nothing but open ice before him when Laycoe, seeing no other choice, wrapped his arms around Richard's shoulders and brought him crashing down to the ice. Referee Red Storey pointed directly to the penalty box, giving Laycoe two minutes to stew and think about how he was going to stop the Rocket next time around, and this next chance proved to be the starting point for the whole affair.

As the Rocket came in on a rush, accelerating down the right side with the puck and preparing for his patented left-turn hook toward the Boston goal, he had one player left to get around—Hal Laycoe. Laycoe reached out with his stick to stop Richard from getting a breakaway. Hal Laycoe grabbed onto the Rocket's waist as Richard somehow carried the defenceman and the puck into the corner. Increasingly frustrated, Laycoe gave up pursuit of the puck and elbowed Richard in the back of the head, slamming him hard into the boards.

"All I know is that on the play in question he had hit me a bad check, and I was trying to get even with him," recalled Richard.

No longer concerned with the play, Richard went after Laycoe. With eyes blazing, Richard punched Laycoe hard in the middle of the ice. As he was falling to the ice, Laycoe swung his stick and hit Richard just above the eye, opening up a bleeding cut that required eight stitches. The sight of blood sent Richard into a frenzy. He dropped his gloves and stick, and clenching his fists, he went straight for Laycoe.

Seeing the rage in the Rocket's eyes, linesman Cliff Thompson tried to restrain Richard, wrenching Richard's arm behind his back in order to stop him from getting at Laycoe. Despite the restraints, Richard kept trying to get at Laycoe, who was now looking for his glasses on the ice. Desperate to get at Laycoe, Richard kept breaking free of Thompson's hold, but the linesman kept tightening his grip from behind. Seeing that Richard was being held back, Laycoe took the opportunity to swing at the Montréal forward.

Richard, increasingly angered by Thompson's repeated efforts to stop him, yelled to the referee, "Stop me from the front but not from behind."

For one last try, Richard broke free and lunged for Laycoe. Thompson again grabbed Richard's arm from behind and held the enraged Canadien back from his prey. But Richard managed to break free and punch Thompson in the face twice. Richard felt the punch was deserved; he had after all given Thompson a warning.

"He wouldn't listen. That's why I hit him."

What is often omitted from the story is that Thompson was once a former Bruins defenceman. Whether this might have been a factor in him holding back Richard from attacking didn't matter in the end since Thompson never officiated another game in the National Hockey League.

For his actions, Richard was thrown out of the game, and Laycoe was given a major penalty and later a misconduct for not getting to the penalty box in due time.

On the train ride back to Montréal, the team was eerily silent. Richard knew he was justified in what he had done, but he hung his head anyway, knowing that he hadn't helped his team.

After the game, Richard was certain that the incident would not garner much attention. He thought he would be suspended for a few games and that would be the end of it. However, the cards were stacked against him. An uproar rang through the media and among league owners that Richard was a loose canon and that he had to be dealt with. It was left to National Hockey League President Clarence Campbell to decide how the Rocket would be punished.

The local French media was in an uproar over having the fate of their hero in the hands of this man, who was known for his dislike of Richard, the Canadiens and all French Canadians in general. It was a theme that was building in the city for some time. The French majority had long been protesting social and wage discrepancies between them and their English counterparts. The city had already seen a number of demonstrations by the French majority, and the Richard affair seemed ready to light the fuse on an already tense situation.

Campbell convened a meeting with Richard, Dick Irvin, Referee Ken Reardon, Hal Laycoe and Bruins Coach Lynn Patrick to review the matter.

Maurice remarked upon entering Campbell's office how he sat at his desk with a smug air of superiority etched on his face. Richard knew that the meeting would not go in his favour. The meeting began with a speech by Bruins Coach Lynn Patrick, who accused Richard of inciting all of the violence.

"Campbell! He has to be reigned in. He's already been reprimanded for one fight. Is this a message that the star players can get away with whatever they damn well choose?" said Patrick, who didn't look Richard in the eyes for the whole meeting.

Richard fought back: "I know I deserve to be punished for what I did, and he [Laycoe] is no angel either. Patrick is not telling it like I remember it," he pleaded in vain.

Campbell had already decided how to deal with the affair, and he wasn't about to change his mind. All of the other teams were angrily calling for a harsh penalty to be handed down to Richard.

In the official 18-paragraph document, Campbell spells out in long form the causes and effects that forced him to suspend Richard. But all the Montréal fans had to read was the final sentence: "In the result, Richard will be suspended from all games, both league and playoff, for the balance of the current season."

When the news hit Montréal, the tension could be felt in the city. The two factions were once again set against each other. French Montréal saw the decision as a direct assault on their hero and on themselves. Montréal West, mainly English, saw the affair as a way of containing the loose canon that the Rocket had become. On the front pages, headlines in the French papers echoed the sentiment that was growing in the city.

La Presse: "Too Harsh a Penalty: Mayor Drapeau hoping for a review of sentence."

Montréal-Matin: "Victim of yet another injustice, the worst ever, Maurice Richard will play no more this season."

At the Richard home, calls started to come in from people he knew and some from people he didn't.

"Rocket! We're going to get even with Campbell. There's going to be a lot of trouble at the Forum tonight!"

"It's an injustice! Campbell will get what is coming to him!"

"Give 'em hell, Maurice!"

Campbell began receiving deaths threats, but he remained firm in his position. He was not about to be bullied. He intended on being present for the next Canadiens game despite the growing animosity.

"It is my right and my duty to be present at the game both as a citizen and as president of the league, and if the mayor or Forum authorities had an apprehension they would not be able to deal with and had requested me to absent myself, I would gladly have complied with their request. No such request was made or even suggested by anyone," said Campbell defiantly.

On the evening of St. Patrick's day, March 17, 1955, the Canadiens were taking on their rivals from Detroit who were just two points behind in the overall standings. Among the 16,000 fans there to watch the game was a very nervous Clarence Campbell, President of the National Hockey League. Outside, angry fans were gathering to chant slogans that denounced Campbell and all those involved: "Campbell, Drop Dead!" "Richard, the Persecuted!" and, "Campbell, Hater of French Canadians!"

Campbell made his appearance midway through the first period, dodging the occasional tomato and verbal punch. With the Red Wings controlling the pace of the game and scoring four goals in the first period, the crowd began to simmer with anger. A young man wearing a leather jacket approached Campbell, ready to give the president of the league a piece of his mind. The young man walked up to Campbell under the pretence of shaking the man's hand but instead punched him three times. Some security guards and police officers rushed the young man and removed him from the Forum.

As the period ended and the teams began to move off the ice, the tense mood in the building was suddenly turned up a notch when someone tossed a tear gas grenade at Campbell. A cloud of harsh smoke filled as patrons made their way toward the exits. At this point, the fury that was taking place inside was carried outside to a crowd of about 10,000 people, setting off the mob that was waiting for an excuse to vent its rage.

The crowd moved eastward down Saint-Catherine and started breaking windows, destroying store-fronts, looting stores, setting fires and overturning police cars. By the time the mob finished venting its anger on Campbell for suspending Richard, west-end downtown Montréal was laid to waste.

Richard was appalled by the violence and destruction that occurred after the game. But inside he sympathized with those who held up banners supporting him. He believed that the whole affair would never have reached the peak that it did had Campbell not made an appearance at the Forum that night.

"What Campbell did was no more sensible than waving a red flag in front of an angry bull," said Richard.

Urged by Frank Selke, General Manager of the Montréal Canadiens, to try and bring a sense of calm to the city, the morning after the riot Richard spoke on the radio in both languages, appealing for an end to the riot. The trouble ceased immediately. But the damage was done, and as the smoke settled on west-end Montréal the city awoke ashamed of what it had done in the name of their hockey hero. Adding insult to injury, the Canadiens went on to lose to the Detroit Red Wings in the Stanley Cup final, and Richard never did get his scoring title.

Maurice Richard recovered from that season, but the scars remained. Campbell robbed him of his chances to win both the Stanley Cup and the scoring title. With Maurice back the next year, the Canadiens finished on top of the league and won the first of five straight Stanley Cups. But the events of 1955 never left the thoughts of Richard and the people of Montréal.

The Plague:
Spanish Influenza Cancels
Stanley Cup

Throughout World War I, soldiers were fighting in trenches across Europe. Confined to these cold trenches, fighting and sleeping in dirty water beside dead or dying soldiers and an army of rats, many soldiers began to develop what appeared to be cold symptoms. As soldiers returned home from the War, an influenza virus began to spread.

Throughout the entire world, over 21 million people died from the Spanish Influenza. In Canada and the United States entire communities were wiped out. In an attempt to minimize the effect of the disease, government officials closed schools. Celebrations and family gatherings were discouraged, and sporting events were shut down.

In only its second year, the National Hockey League faced a major roadblock to establishing itself in North America. The Spanish Influenza began to affect not only the players but also the large number of people who came to watch the games. Attendance at the games dropped greatly because of government warnings to avoid public gatherings. Banners were plastered all over the cities warning people how to avoid contracting the virus. Panic rolled across the country as families and communities began to break up because of the number of cases that developed.

The players and teams in the NHL were not immune to the disease either.

At the beginning of the 1918–19 season, the NHL only managed to sign up three teams, with a chance for the winner to play against the rival league of the Pacific Coast Hockey Association. The teams were the Ottawa Senators, the Montréal Canadiens and the Toronto Arenas. But halfway through this early season, the Toronto Arenas withdrew from the league because of financial problems, and the league was forced to play a best of seven series between the remaining Senators and Canadiens, with the winner to battle the Seattle Metropolitans, winner of the PCHA title.

Led by Newsy Lalonde, the Canadiens proved to be the winners as they easily beat the Senators four games to one. While preparing for their battle against Seattle, several Canadiens players fell ill. At first, most thought it was the common cold, but the symptoms progressed, and by the time the final game—which was scheduled for April 1, 1919— came around, several of the players had become seriously ill.

It was believed that the Canadiens players picked up the illness while in Seattle for their first game of the finals. Returning to Montréal, Newsy Lalonde, Joe Hall, Louis Berlinquette and owner George Kennedy fell ill with influenza, leaving Odie Cleghorn, Georges Vezina and Didier Pitre as the only players healthy enough to skate. The Seattle team arrived in Montréal with seven players in the recovery stage of the virus, all in bed at the same time. Rumours began to spread among the ill players that it was because they played so hard to get to the finals that their bodies became weak and thus more susceptible to the disease.

With more and more players becoming violently ill from the epidemic, the decision came down from NHL management on April 1 (just before the start of the final game in the Stanley Cup playoffs) that the game was cancelled, and because the series was tied, no winner would be declared. Four days after the decision to cancel the playoffs, Canadiens star "Bad Joe" Hall lost his life to the influenza virus in a Seattle hospital, proving that the league did the right thing in cancelling the playoffs and potentially saving lives. That was the only time in the history of the NHL that a Stanley Cup champion has never been crowned.

The Longest Game in NHL History

The first hockey game of the 1936 playoffs saw defending Stanley Cup champions the Montréal Maroons taking on their season rivals the Detroit Red Wings in a best of five series. The match was expected to be a defensive-style game and only drew a crowd of 9000 fans.

The game started out very physical, with both teams hitting hard trying to set the tone for the series early. Instead of an offensive back and forth game the crowd was treated to a defensive tussle that had the goaltenders and the defencemen deciding the pace of the game. Maroons goaltender Lorne Chabot and Red Wings goalie Normie Smith had their work cut out for them as they were pelted with a constant barrage of shots, but both were having the game of their season. They stopped everything that came their way.

After three intense periods of a doggedly fought defensive struggle where caution was the overall theme of the game, both teams went back to their dressing rooms trying to figure out a way to get past the other team's defences.

Five minutes into the first overtime period, the fans knew that both teams hadn't figured out any way through each other's respective defensive strategies, and that the game might well have the makings of a drawn-out battle as the two goaltenders almost stood on their heads to make saves. It was Red Wings goaltender Normie Smith who stole the show from Chabot; Smith faced 46 shots by the time the first overtime finished. The Maroons poured on the offence at the end of the first period, trying to wear the young goaltender down, but somehow, Smith managed to stop everything that was sent his way. Five more overtime periods passed by in this manner, and radio announcers began to joke that the Forum should install beds for fans at the next game.

Although the goaltenders deserve most of the accolades for their outstanding efforts, it was a rookie Detroit forward that would be remembered as the one who ended the longest game in National Hockey League history.

Modere Bruneteau had been called up to the Detroit Red Wings just two weeks earlier and was still in the process of getting to know the pace of the NHL when he was thrown into his first playoff series. By the end of the fifth overtime, he thought the game would go on forever or else he was going to lose all feeling in his legs and just would not be able to complete the game. But the coaches were watching, and Bruneteau wanted to make a good impression in his first playoff game.

"All right!" screamed Detroit Red Wings Coach Jack Adams. "Who has enough spit left in their legs to get out there and finish this game so these good people can go home to their families? This is a game we should win. Let's give Normie the break he deserves for keeping you guys in this game and put an end to this."

Leaving the dressing room inspired, Bruneteau hit the ice with a renewed and strong sense of energy. However, it took another 17 minutes to break the Maroons defence and the wall their goaltender Chabot was putting up.

Detroit forward Hec Kilrea got hold of the puck and made his way toward the Montréal Maroons net, hoping to find a hole that Chabot might have left in a moment of weakness. Letting a shot go from about five metres out in front of the net, he hit a Maroons defenceman, and the puck rolled dangerously in front of Chabot. Rookie Bruneteau, seeing the puck open, rushed to the middle of the ice and took a wild stab at the puck, which trickled past a startled Chabot and into the back of the net. The crowd paused, not knowing whether to boo the Red Wings for beating their home team or cheer them for finally ending the game at 2:25 AM. As Bruneteau celebrated his goal the Maroons slowly made their way off the ice, despondent that they lost a long-fought battle, but a little relieved that the game was finally over.

In the end, Smith faced 90 shots compared to Chabot's 68 in 176.5 total minutes. The previous record was set between the Toronto Maple Leafs and the Boston Bruins at 104.46 minutes in the 1933 playoffs. Bruneteau secured a place on the team, and the Red Wings went on to win the series and the Stanley Cup. No teams have since played a longer game in the history of the National Hockey League.

Death by Hockey
Murder on Ice

Most people tend to view the early days of hockey as a time when the game was in its purest form, played by gentlemen pursuing a gentlemanly sport. However, the early days of hockey were nowhere near the friendly game that some like to remember. The life of a hockey player before the formation of the professional leagues was filled with broken bones, stitches and fights, fights and more fights.

Since it was not uncommon for some teams to play each other several times during a season, the rivalries between some cities grew to be legendary. In the battle for bragging rights, players and fans often solved their disputes with their fists instead of the score sheet. It was a rough game played by rough men, and many times hockey careers were cut short because of injury. However, the violence never grew out of control, and rivalries were often settled with a couple of punches and a pat on the back. But on a dark and cold March night in 1907, during a game between the Ottawa Victorias and the Cornwall Hockey Club of the Federal Amateur Hockey league, the violence got out of hand.

The animosity between the two teams could be felt before the first puck was dropped. Ottawa was the dominant team in the league, and that season they had already handed Cornwall several embarrassing losses. But this time, Cornwall was ready for them, and their plan was to come out hitting hard.

The game was quiet for the first half but by the time the second half started, several players were taking runs at each other and the expletives began to fly across the arena. Cornwall forward Owen McCourt took it upon himself to pick up the tempo of the game by making several runs at the Ottawa players. His target of choice that night was Ottawa's Arthur Throop.

As the game went on, the two players exchanged both verbal and physical punches. The antagonism reached its peak when Throop took McCourt hard into the boards. After McCourt shook off the hit, he skated directly for Throop with his stick raised above his shoulders and the obvious intent of doing harm to Throop. McCourt swung his stick at Throop, hitting him right above the eye and opening a 10-centimetre gash that bled all over the ice. The benches cleared, and the ice was soon full of players scrambling to get at McCourt.

Ottawa forward Charles Masson, who just saw his teammate fall to the ice bleeding, went straight for McCourt and delivered a similar blow to the head with his stick. Unfortunately, the stick caught McCourt on the temple and sent him crashing to the ice. Masson, not thinking that the blow to the head seriously injured McCourt, continued his assault on the Cornwall players. He took Captain Reddy McMillan into the boards with both players' sticks flying in the air. It wasn't until the referee got everything under control that they realized McCourt was still laid out on the ice and wasn't moving.

After McCourt was carried off the ice, the game resumed. To everyone's surprise McCourt made his way back onto the ice but only played for five more minutes before being taken back to the dressing room. It wasn't until about 30 minutes later that McCourt began to feel dizzy and confused. The trainer rushed him to the hospital, and on the way there, McCourt passed out and never woke up. He died two days later in hospital from a severe brain haemorrhage caused by a blow to the head.

Everybody was stunned at McCourt's death because he had continued to play after the hit from Masson. The referee said afterward that he had even joked with the Cornwall forward after he came back on the ice.

"I did not think he was very seriously hurt, however, because during the time he was playing after his first absence he seemed to be all right. Once I collided with him and his skate caught in the leg of my trousers and made a hole there, and I told him, jokingly, that if he was not more careful I would have to charge him for a new pair of trousers, and he replied, 'All right.'"

After the news got out that McCourt died from the injuries he received during the game, local police issued a warrant charging Charles Masson with McCourt's murder.

It came out in the ensuing trial that McCourt had received several knocks to the head during the game, so the evidence was inconclusive as to who delivered the fatal blow. The referee noticed that when McCourt came back after the initial blow to the head by Masson, he had several cuts and bruises around his ears and forehead, and the referee was sure that those were the result of the Masson attack. Due to the lack of sufficient evidence Masson was acquitted on all murder charges and set free.

The Federal Amateur Hockey League only lasted another season before it folded because of other leagues that were directly competing against it.

Bill Mosienko
21 Seconds of Glory

It was not the Chicago Blackhawks' greatest hockey season. During the 1951–52 season, the team posted the worst record in the NHL, and empty seats at their arena showed that the fans had lost faith in their team after several straight-losing seasons. The Blackhawks were not going to make the playoffs, and the glory days of Bobby Hull were still several years away. The only ray of sunshine in the Chicago locker room was a 173-centimetre, 73-kilogram right-winger named Bill Mosienko.

Since the early 1940s, Mosienko had been a strong, solid forward who could score goals and play a solid defensive game when called upon. The team hoped Mosienko would develop into a goal-scoring star that could compete with the other contemporaries such as Maurice Richard and Gordie Howe. But Mosienko could never reach that level on a team that struggled to stay out of the bottom of the division for most of his 14-year career with them.

Despite the odds stacked against him, Mosienko's best year came in the 1951–52 season. He ended the season seventh overall in scoring, and on March 23, 1952 (the last game of the regular season), Mosienko secured himself a place in the history books.

Just over 3000 people gathered at Madison Square Garden that night to watch the fifth-place

Rangers take on the last-place Blackhawks. The game meant nothing in the overall standings since both teams were eliminated from the play-offs; the game was for bragging rights. Both teams were having difficulty winning games that season, and the crowd's silence showed that the fans had lost interest.

The game started out like any other as both teams played an evenly matched game. The first period ended with the Rangers leading by one goal. With no penalties called, the crowd was treated to an open-ended game with equal chances to score coming to both teams. But by the end of the second period, the Rangers opened up their lead to three goals with the score set at 5–2 for the start of the third period.

In the Chicago dressing room, the mood was less than jubilant because they faced a three-goal deficit to a team they just could not beat that season. Chicago Coach Eddie Goodfellow paced the locker room floor, looked over his losing team and tried to find some inspirational words to motivate them, anything to keep his team from ending the season on a losing note.

"I know this hasn't been the greatest season, guys, but this doesn't mean we have to give up. The Rangers aren't any better than we are. They are playing the type of game that we thrive in, so why aren't we the ones with the lead?" Goodfellow asked. "All we need to do is start connecting some passes and running our system and things will definitely turn our way in the third. You'll see! Heck I even bet my job on it!" (Ironically, Eddie Goodfellow never coached in the National Hockey League again.)

The Blackhawks didn't exactly come out of the dressing room inspired by Goodfellow's words, and the Rangers quickly added to their lead with a goal by forward Eddie Slowinski. The goal was no doubt the catalyst that needed to be set under the Blackhawks forwards, who came out flying in the sixth minute of the period...led by Bill Mosienko.

At 5:59 of the third period the linesman dropped the puck for a face-off in the Blackhawks zone. Scrambling for the puck, Blackhawks centre Gus Bodnar got it and made his way to centre ice. He caught Mosienko with a nice saucer pass as he was coming down through the neutral zone. With two Rangers defencemen blocking his way over the blue line, Mosienko let loose a shot from just above the blue line; it beat stunned Rangers rookie netminder Lorne Anderson at 6:09 in the third period. Mosienko stayed on the ice for the next face-off at centre ice. Bodnar won the face-off again and got the puck to Mosienko, who was already sneaking down the right side hoping to catch the defence sleeping. He cut across the middle and fired a quick snap shot that found the back of the net.

Mosienko scored his second goal at 6:20. And the next face-off unfolded the same way; Bodnar got control of the puck and caught Mosienko with a beautiful pass that sent him flying into the Rangers zone. From the top of the circle, Mosienko fired a shot that would have fooled the best goalie in the league for his third goal at 6:30. Mosienko scored a hat trick in 21 seconds, eclipsing the old record of one minute and four seconds established by Carl Liscombe of the Detroit Red Wings in 1938.

The crowd awoke with a volume that seemed to come from twice their number once it was announced over the loudspeaker that Mosienko just established a new NHL record. Back on the Chicago bench, Coach Goodfellow went over and congratulated Mosienko on the three goals.

"Must have been my little speech that inspired you out there, eh Mosy!" said Goodfellow jokingly.

Cracking a smile, Mosienko looked at his coach. "Yeah, must have been!" he said with a hint of sarcasm.

With the momentum shifted to the Blackhawks, they went on to stun the Rangers by scoring two more goals to win the game by a final score of 7–6. As the teams cleared the ice at the end of the game, the Rangers fans respectfully gave Bill Mosienko a round of applause.

A decade after his retirement from the NHL, Mosienko was inducted into the Hockey Hall of Fame and to this day remains the holder of the record for the three fastest goals.

Chapter Six

THE
SCORE SHEET

To avoid any arguments about who might be the best forward, defenceman or goaltender, sometimes it's just best to let the statistics speak for themselves.

All statistics taken from:

www.statshockey.homestead.com

All-Time Number of Games Played

1. Gordie Howe   1767

2. Mark Messier   1756

3. Ron Francis   1729

4. Scott Stevens   1635

5. Larry Murphy   1615

6. Ray Bourque   1612

7. Dave Andreychuk   1595

8. Alex Delvecchio   1550

9. Johnny Bucyk   1540

10. Phil Housley   1495

All-Time Points Leaders

1. Wayne Gretzky 2857

2. Mark Messier 1887

3. Gordie Howe 1850

4. Ron Francis 1795

5. Marcel Dionne 1771

6. Steve Yzerman 1721

7. Mario Lemieux 1701

8. Phil Esposito 1590

9. Ray Bourque 1579

10. Paul Coffey 1531

All-Time
Goals Leaders

1. Wayne Gretzky   894

2. Gordie Howe   801

3. Brett Hull   741

4. Marcel Dionne   731

5. Phil Esposito   717

6. Mike Gartner   708

7. Mark Messier   694

8. Mario Lemieux   683

9. Steve Yzerman   678

10. Luc Robitaille   653

All-Time Assists Leaders

1. Wayne Gretzky 1963

2. Ron Francis 1247

3. Mark Messier 1193

4. Ray Bourque 1169

5. Paul Coffey 1135

6. Adam Oates 1063

7. Gordie Howe 1049

8. Steve Yzerman 1043

9. Marcel Dionne 1040

10. Mario Lemieux 1018

All-Time Goaltender Win Leaders

1. Patrick Roy   551

2. Terry Sawchuk   447

3. Jacques Plante   435

4. Ed Belfour   433

5. Tony Esposito   423

6. Glenn Hall   407

7. Grant Fuhr   403

8. Martin Brodeur   402

9. Curtis Joseph   396

10. Mike Vernon   385

All-Time
Shutout Leaders

1. Terry Sawchuk   103

2. George Hainsworth   94

3. Glenn Hall   84

4. Jacques Plante   82

5. Tiny Thompson   81

6. Alex Connell   81

7. Tony Espositio   76

8. Martin Brodeur   75

9. Lorne Chabot   73

10. Ed Belfour   73

All-Time
Penalty Leaders

1. Dave "Tiger" Williams   3966

2. Dale Hunter   3565

3. Tie Domi   3406

4. Marty McSorley   3381

5. Bob Probert   3300

6. Rob Ray   3201

7. Craig Berube   3149

8. Tim Hunter   3142

9. Chris Nilan   3043

10. Rick Toccet   2970

NOTES ON SOURCES

Carrier, Roch. *Our Life With the Rocket: The Maurice Richard Story*. Toronto: Viking Press, 2001.

Diamond, Dan (ed). *The Official National Hockey League 75th Anniversary Commemorative Book*. Toronto: McClelland & Stewart Inc., 1991.

Diamond, Dan (ed). *Total Hockey*. New York: Total Sports Publishing, 1998.

Dryden, Steve. *The Magic, The Legend, The Numbers: Total Gretzky*. Toronto: McClelland & Stewart Inc., 1999.

Goyens, Chrys and Frank Orr. *Maurice Richard: Reluctant Hero*. Montréal: Team Power Pub, 2000.

Gretzky, Walter and Jim Taylor. *Gretzky: From the Backyard Rink to the Stanley Cup*. New York: Avon Books, 1984.

Hunt, Jim. *The Men in the Nets*. Toronto: McGraw-Hill Limited, 1972.

McDonell, Chris. *100 Hockey Star Stories*. Buffalo: Firefly Books, 2002.

———. *Shooting from the Lip: Hockey's Best Quotes and Quips*. Buffalo: Firefly Books, 2004.

Melrose, Barry et al. *Wayne Gretzky: The Making of the Great One*. Dallas: Beckett Publications, 1998.

Morrison, Scott. *The Days Canada Stood Still: Canada vs. USSR 1972*. Toronto: McGraw-Hill Ryerson Limited, 1989.

Richard, Maurice and Stan Fischler. *The Flying Frenchmen: Hockey's Greatest Dynasty*. New York: Hawthorn Books Inc., 1971.

Young, Scott. *Hello Canada! The Life and Times of Foster Hewitt*. Toronto: Seal Books, 1985.